Legal Stuff

Copyright & Legal Information

PRINCE® - "PRINCE®" is a (registered) Trade Mark of AXELOS Limited. All rights reserved.

Dedication

Whilst writing this book my father became critically ill, the doctors brought my family together to say he wouldn't pull through and we needed to say goodbye.

Which, to anyone who knows my father is a mistake, he is too stubborn to ever let a doctor be right and pulled through. However, in truth this was only possible because of the amazing work undertaken by the doctors, nurses and staff on his ward in a hospital in Tameside England – Thank You from the bottom of my heart for your amazing work

My father is my hero and whilst he is a stubborn sod, I could never imagine him not being in my life, and I know all of my brothers feel the same way

Introduction

Prince2 – is an abbreviation of **Pr**ojects **in** **C**ontrolled **E**nvironments and is classed as one of the leading project management methodologies and is internationally recognised.

It has been improved over a number of decades by a team of highly experienced Project Managers from different fields, which helps ensure Prince2 remains a methodology that is not tied or linked any particular industry type or field, again ensuring I remains a generic methodology

Prince was originally developed to be used in IT projects in the public sector within the UK, however with the launch of Prince2 in 1996, it became available to use for any project and was licensed for the use within any project type or industry,

For a long period of time, APMG was the accreditor for Prince2, however this was transitioned to AXELOS, which is a joint venture between the Cabinet Office and Capita

This book is not intended as a replacement to either the manual of any official training provided to support you obtaining the Prince2 qualification, it is intended as an introduction and a way of introducing you to Prince2 and the methodology and to support you through your learning.

The aim of the book is to highlight the fundamental aspects of Pricne2 and to provide simple, clean explanations and diagrams. The main aim is to show how the elements of Prince2 integrate together and you with a provide a boarder understanding. This book should be useful too as a pre-cursor to the training whether that is on-line, or classroom based, and especially supportive for those who are undertaking the journey using self-study, or even for those Project Managers who are already in the field but need a refresher on Prince2 2017 or the methodology without the need for formal accreditation

It doesn't focus upon passing the exam or provide any tips on the exams themselves.

When I teach Prince2, I explain that Project Management is basically based upon common sense and good communication, the use and practice of Prince2 2017 is effectively the use of a structure and the use of a standard terminology that provides a common language.

A favourite quote I like to use,

> "If you can't explain it simply, you don't understand it well enough!!"
> *Albert Einstein*

Which is true in so many ways, I have worked with numerous people who have been instructors, or subject matter experts but they simply don't know the subject well enough to be able to explain it both simply and in a way that actually makes the methodology of Prince2 2017 and the art of Project Management either interesting or fun

This book is purposefully written to be both informal and to make the subject less "dry" and more interesting and hopefully more sense

1 - The Business Case and its importance

The Business Case is effectively one of the most important documents and provides the information on why the project is being undertaken, what the aims of the project are, however before it can be produced, the objectives need to be understood, these are then recorded within the Business Case.

There are 6 objectives within Prince2, these can also be known as project variables or performance targets. These are:

1. Time
2. Cost
3. Quality
4. Scope
5. Risk
6. Benefits

The 6 Project Objectives

Each project will define the objectives which are expected to be met by the end of the project. The role of the project manager is to achieve these objectives within expected performance targets. These performance targets are: cost, time, scope, quality, risk and benefits

Time – How long is the project, how long before the project realises the benefits identified. As the Project Manager you don't have to be a subject matter expert, and often you're not going to be a subject matter expert, which raises the importance of having access to the relevant subject matter experts to support the understanding of the time needed for the project and provide a rough estimate of the time needed

Cost – How much is the project going to cost (to both delver and to maintain), understanding the cost of the project at the earlier stages can often be an estimate and again needs input from subject matter experts or even suppliers. This allows the project to be started on more of a realistic estimate rather than just guesswork.

Quality – What is the organisation trying to achieve in relation to the final product (also known as a deliverable, output or specialist product). Is it a new system, a service or a building. This will be part of the information (hopefully) contained within the Project Mandate, however this will need further clarification between the Project Manager and members of the Project Team. This information is often at a level that is too high to be effective and can be vague, this information needs to be elaborated and turned into more measurable (also known as tangible) acceptance criteria as early in the project as possible

Scope – Scope links perfectly into the objectives related to Quality, this ensures there is a total understanding of the quality expectations and that there is no confusion between the users of the projects products (outputs) and the suppliers who will create them. It is also crucial to define what is not within the scope of the project and again, ensure there is no confusion

Risks – Projects by their very nature, introduce change, which introduces uncertainty, which is effectively introducing risk. There is no way to remove risk from projects, risks need to be managed as early as possible and the process of Identification relating to major risks that could affect the realisation of the objectives, and therefore possibly impacting the justification of the project, but also the management of risks at a lower level and not just focusing upon the major risks

Benefits – In the most simplistic terms, benefits are what is to be gained from the projects products (outputs). In the majority of projects, these are financially based and measurable in either cost savings or revenue generation or a mix of both. Prince2 makes the statement that in most projects these benefits will be realised after the project has been completed and the project product starts to provide the change within the organisation and produces these benefits. However, this is not the case in all projects, benefits can be achieved in projects incrementally and as such the benefits can start to be measured whilst the project is still ongoing

All of the details relating to objectives of the project are documented within the Business Case as part of the overall project justification, and are used to assess the Continued Business Justification of the project throughout its lifecycle

The Golden Triangle – Time, Cost, Quality

The Project Mandate, is often vague and contains only the minimum of information about the project and what is to be delivered. It often contains no real information in relation to numbers, and this is how projects often begin with little or no information relating to time or cost

Adversely, in some organisations the mandate contains strict time and cost information that are set and information on the project products (outputs), in this situation, the process of documenting the Time, Cost and Scope is relatively easy as this is already provided, however it is worth reviewing this again with subject matter experts to assess the Time, Cost to understand if these figures are realistic (often this information is low, and unachievable)

The golden triangle is a balancing act, it is key to ensure that the triangle is clearly understand and that the scope, time are representative of the cost, if these are misaligned there is little chance to deliver the project, for example if the project has a high scope, little time and is underfunded, the project manager (or a seasoned project manager) will know that this is a constraint or a risk to the overall success of the project and the chances of success are minimal at best

The Business Case and the viability of the project

So, what is meant when we say the viability of the project or a viable business case.

This is a term used where the projects benefits are positive or outweigh the costs associated with the costs to deliver and support the projects products (outputs). The investment in relation to both costs and time should be clearly understood and documented along with the benefits associated with the projects products. It is often thought of as a "Cost-Benefit analysis", this is where projects that have measurable financial benefits are often easier to gain approval for

The assumption is that the Project Mandate is provided because the project is already determined to have a positive business case where the identified or assumed benefits outweigh the costs to deliver and maintain the projects products (outputs)

The Business Case is not a static document (contrary to some organisations and their processes), within a Prince2 2017 project, the business case is regularly reviewed and reassessed to confirm the project remains justified (its Continued Business Justification).

It is reviewed as part of the Managing Stage Boundary Process (SB) and updated to reflect the most up to date and accurate information particularly in relation to time and costs. The Business Case is also reviewed when any risks, issues and changes are raised that could affect the achievement of the projects objectives (Time, Cost, Scope, Quality, benefits and Risk)

In most projects, it's a sad truth that estimates for time and cost often go up and not down when the project is in progress, this is often the case in longer projects. These estimates should be revisited, especially in relation to the benefits when impacted by external conditions. As a result, the question of the benefits and whether they still outweigh the investment to deliver the projects products in relation to time and costs and the risks associated with the delivery

However, what happens if the benefits are not financially based or financially measurable?

In this scenario the Business Case is based more upon the non-financial benefits, and these reasons become more important and need to be clearly defined and documented. It is important to also continually revisit these and ensure the project remains viable

If the Business Case becomes no longer valid, and therefore the project is no longer justifiable (unless it can be changed by a major change in scope) the organisation should stop the project and have the courage to actually make the decision to prematurely close the project and stop using resources (systems, services, resources, money) to deliver a project that could potentially deliver little or no benefits, and the cost to deliver will outweigh the benefits especially if these resources could be used on more justifiable projects

However, this isn't always done, in most organisations once a project starts it will continue irrespective of the justification and if it remains valid, projects become political and cancelling or closing a project prematurely can be seen a failure, when in essence the fact that it continues is the failure and closing it should be seen as a successful use of the methodology and the process

2 - The Structure of Prince2
The Prince2 methodology is made up of four integrated elements,
1. Principles
2. Themes
3. Processes
4. The Project Environment

The Principles	The guiding obligations and best practices All 7 Principles need to be applied to a Prince2 Project One of the principles is that Prince2 should be tailored to make it appropriate to the project
The Themes	The 7 aspects of Project Management that must be applied throughout the life of the project
The Processes	The 7 steps in the project lifecycle The processes describe a progression from Pre-Project to Closure, each process has checklists of recommended activities, products and related responsibilities
The Project Environment	The flexibility to tailor Prince2 the Project to meet the project or organisations needs

The 7 Principles of Prince2

Prince derives its methods from 7 core principles. Collectively, these principles provide a framework for good practice and are the basis for Prince2 2017 being a generic methodology that can be used on any type of project. These 7 Principles are:

1. **Continued Business Justification** - A project must make good business sense. There needs to be a clear return on investment and the use of time and resources should be justified
2. **Learn from Experience** - Project teams should take lessons from previous projects into account. A lessons log is kept updated for this purpose
3. **Define Roles and Responsibilities** - Everyone involved in a project should know what they and others are doing and what is expected of them. This includes knowing who the decision makers are
4. **Manage by Stages** - Difficult tasks are better off broken into manageable chunks, or as Prince2 2017 calls them, Management Stages
5. **Manage by Exception** - A project running well doesn't need a lot of intervention from management. The project board is only informed if there is or might be a problem that requires their direction or a decision making
6. **Focus on Products** - Everyone should know ahead of time what's expected of the product. Product requirements determine work activity, not the other way around
7. **Tailor to the Environment** - PRINCE2 can be scaled and tailored

Projects that adapt Prince2 2017 to their needs are more likely to succeed than projects that use Prince2 2017 dogmatically and with no tailoring. It is crucial that the project follows all 7 of the principles, failure to follow these principles means the project is not being managed as a Prince2 2017 project

The 7 Themes of Prince2

Themes provide insight into how the project should be managed. They can be thought of as continual knowledge areas, or how the 7 principles are put into practice. They are set up at the beginning of the project and then managed and monitored throughout its lifecycle. Projects are kept on track by constantly addressing these themes:

1. **Business Case -** Related to the Continued Business Justification Principle. This theme provides knowledge about whether a project is worthwhile and achievable and supports the assessment of its continued viability
2. **Organisation** - Related to the Defined Roles and Responsibilities Principle. The organisation theme requires project managers to have everyone's roles and responsibilities on record

3. **Quality** - Related to the Focus on Products Principle. Quality can be an abstract concept, so defining it at the beginning of a project is vital to keeping the work on track
4. **Plans** - A plan describes how targets will be achieved. It focuses on the products, timescale, cost, quality and benefits
5. **Risk** - The purpose of this theme is to identify, assess and control any uncertain events during the projects lifecycle. These are recorded in a risk register. Negative risks are called threats and positive ones are called opportunities
6. **Change** - This theme is about handling change requests and issues that arise during the project. The idea is not to prevent changes, but to get them agreed on before they're executed and ensure only the right changes are both approved and controlled
7. **Progress** - Progress is about tracking the project. This allows project managers to check and control where they are relative to the plans (project Plan, Stage Plan and Team Plan). Not only can projects go off the rails without this – or any one of the themes, but by not tracking, you may not even be aware that it's happening and when you do realise, it will invariably be too late

The 7 Processes of Prince2

The Prince2 2017 method also separates the running of a project into 7 processes. Each one is overseen by the project manager and approved by the project board. Here is a breakdown of each stage:

1. **Starting Up a Project (SU)**
    - Create a project mandate, which answers logistical questions about the project. It explains the purpose of the project, who will carry it out and how to execute it.
    - A project brief is derived from the mandate, lessons log and discussions with people involved in the project.
    - A team is assigned and with the brief, they should have all the information needed for next process.
2. **Initiating a Project (IP)** - This stage is about realising what needs to be done to complete the project. The project manager outlines how the following performance targets will be managed:
    - Time
    - Cost
    - Quality
    - Scope
    - Benefits
    - Risk
3. **Directing a Project (DP)** - This is an ongoing process from the beginning to the end of a project. The project board manages these activities:
    - Initiation
    - Stage boundaries
    - Ad hoc direction/guidance
    - Project closure
4. **Controlling a Stage (CS)** - Project managers authorise work packages, which break the project down into manageable activities. These are assigned to teams and their managers. The project manager then has these tasks:

- Overseeing and reporting on work package progress
- Stepping in to correct problems
- The team manager, meanwhile has these tasks:
- Coordinating daily work
- Communicating between team members and the project manager

5. **Managing Product Delivery (MP)** - This is how the communication between the team manager and project manager is controlled. MP consists of these activities:
   - Accepting a work package
   - Executing a work package
   - Delivering a work package

6. **Managing Stage Boundaries (SB)** - Project managers and the board review every stage. The board decides whether to continue the project. The project manager meets with the team to record lessons learned for the next stage. SB consists of these activities:
   - Plan the next stage
   - Update the project plan
   - Update the business case
   - Report the stage end or produce an exception plan

7. **Managing Stage Boundaries (SB)**
   - Decommission the project
   - Identify follow-on actions
   - Prepare benefits and project evaluation reviews
   - Free up leftover resources
   - Hand over products to the customer

The Project Environment

The Project Environment comprises of all of the organisational influences upon the project, such as the BAU processes, the corporate standards etc as well as any legislative or other external factors that may impact or be relevant to the project.

This should be considered when deciding how to tailor Prince2 and the methodology in relation to both the organisation and the project, we will go through this in more detail later in the book

Prince2 Products – Specialist and Management Products

Although the products are not part of the integrated elements of Prince2, Prince2 is focused upon products is a key part of the success in relation to Prince2 and a Prince2 project

Management Products – In a Prince2 project, management products are information sets that are presented in a variety of forms – not necessarily just as documents. Management products are incorporated in the PRINCE2 ® processes to enable the various roles that make up a project management team to take action and make decisions

Prince2 distinguishes between three different types of management products:

Baseline Management Products define certain aspects of the project and are subject to change control once approved

For example: Business Case, Product Descriptions, strategies, Project Initiation Documentation, plans, etc

Records are dynamic management products. They contain information on project progress.
For example: Logs (e.g. Daily Log), registers (Quality Register, Risk Register, Issue Register), etc

Reports provide a snapshot of specific aspects of the project.
For example: Highlight Report, End Stage Report, Exception Report, End Project Report, etc

Management Products vs. Specialist Products

Management products are one of the key features that enable a project to be "managed". They should only be applied where appropriate and are therefore subject to tailoring.

The official manual "Managing Successful Projects with Prince2 contains Product Descriptions for a total of 26 management products. The Product Descriptions include the purpose and composition of each management product together with information on its contents, as well as the quality criteria that must be taken into consideration when creating it

A clear distinction should be made between management products and specialist products.

Specialist products are the products that make up the final deliverable of a project. The production of one or more specialist products is defined in the relevant plan. Prince2 focuses on the project management of these

Specialists products may be tangible, for example a new product, or a building, or they may be intangible, software, a new or revised business process or a project may involve a mix of the two

Tailoring Prince2

When I taught the older version of Prince2 (Prince2 2009), the feedback or comments would often be that it was bureaucratic or that it was too unwieldly to be used on anything other than large projects, there are too many documents, its simply overkill

Prince2 has this reputation, however in truth its mainly because there was a misunderstanding or not enough knowledge of Prince2, Tailoring has always been built into Prince2, but with the updates in Prince2 2017 it has become a more embedded part of the methodology, along with a chapter that focuses upon the tailoring of the methodology in relation to the organisation,

The main areas that should considered in relation to tailoring are:
- Simple projects that have little risk, low duration, low cost etc
- Projects that use the Agile methodology
- Projects that involve external suppliers
- Projects that involve multiple owners or sponsors
- Projects that are part of a larger program

This all means that there is little excuse for not understanding the options to tailor Prince2. The most obvious factor when considering the tailoring of Prince2 that will influence the formality with which to use the method on any project irrespective of its scale or complexity (measured in relation to the budget, timescale, number of people, complexity, risk etc)

This tailoring will be relative to the size of the organisation that is delivering the project, what one organisation considers small and simple another organisation would consider large or complex. Whilst it should be common sense not to adopt the same level of formality for small, simple projects as that of large, complex projects, this is not always the case

Later in the book, we will demonstrate how to deliver a project using the minimum of people and documents to show that Prince2 can be tailored and that it is not overly bureaucratic

Prince2 – What does it mean to use Prince2
Whilst Prince2 is massively flexible and can be tailored, there are a clearly defined set of minimum requirements that are needed to say that a project is being ran as a Prince2 project and following the methodology

These are:
- That the 7 Principles are being applied
- That the 7 Themes are being used and the minimum requirements are being met for the 7 Themes
- That the project is either using the recommended Prince2 techniques within each theme or using the alternative or equivalent techniques
- The processes used satisfy the purpose and objectives (even if they are simplified, combined or even omitted)

How the integrated elements fit together
This is often the area that is the most confusing for delegates when I am training, there first experience is a huge manual, with a language of its own and a set of "elements" that are integrated but there nothing showing the integration between them in one clean, simple place within the methodology

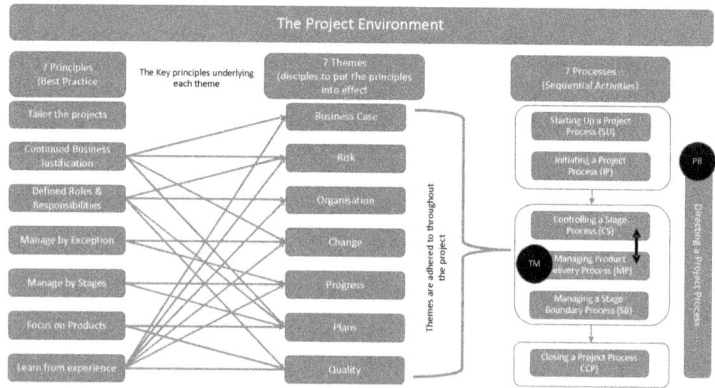

Figure 1 - Prince2 2017 Integrated Elements

Figure 1 shows the integration between the elements of Prince2 in the most effective way of presenting the integration between the Principles, Themes, Processes and The Project Environment

The most obvious relationships between the Principles on the left hand of Figure 1 and the Themes and how they are put into effect in the middle column of Figure 1, represented using the links (arrows) between the 2 areas. Tailoring is part of the entire Project Lifecycle and can be applied to any Theme or Process, hence it is not a separate area or consideration

Continued Business Justification – The Business Case must remain viable throughout the life of the project, otherwise the project should be stopped. It fundamentally links to the Business Case Theme.

There is also a strong link or relationship between the Continued Business Justification Principle and the Risk Theme, Risk is effectively about controlling uncertainty, whilst you cannot stop risks within a project purely because the very nature of a project is to introduce change. Risks that are classified as Major Risks are those that could impact the projects ability to achieve its identified objectives and cause the project to no longer be justifiable. These risks are recorded within the Business Case, no matter the size of the project, there will always be risks and there will always be risks that could impact the viability of the project or question the projects total viability

Defined Roles & Responsibilities – Projects involve people (of course!!!), these people should have a clear understanding of their roles and responsibilities and of course the roles and responsibilities of others within the project. This principle is at the very core of Prince2 (and one of the reasons for its success).

This is an ideal point to review the four levels of management within the Project:

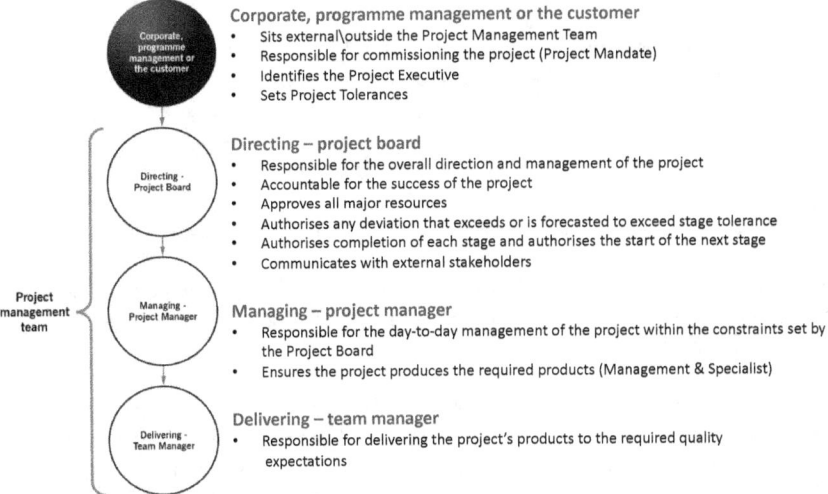

Figure 2 - Project Management Structure

Corporate, Programme Management or Customer – Effectively act as the sponsors of the project and provide it with the mandate (the trigger). If the project is part of a programme, the project acts as the umbrella for the project.

The Programme will have Programme Board and a Business Case already approved and the Project will become part of the Programme and its structure

If a Project is not part of a Programme, if it is standalone, there is a still a layer of Corporate Management above the Project Board that allows for escalation by the Project Board

If you are the looking at the project from the supplier's perspective, the organisation that is paying for the project is effectively the customer

The Project Board – Is made up of 3 roles and each role must be represented, they can be combined (and we will discuss these options later)

    The Executive – has the accountability for the projects overall success or failure and has the deciding vote. The Project Board is not a democracy, the Executive has the final say. The Execute represents the Business interests on the project in relation to the financial aspects of the project and is focused upon ensuring the project is value for money and it will deliver a return of investment. The Executive is often part of Corporate, Programme or Customer

    Senior User – Represents the interests of the users (the community who will use the specialist products (outputs) of the project. The Senior User will help define the requirements, providing information on what the customers quality expectations are allowing the acceptance criteria to be aligned and prioritised.

    The Senior User will also provide information in relation to the benefits, how they will be reported upon and by whom.

    Senior Supplier – is representing the supplier interests. The Suppliers are the organisations, people or teams who are creating the specialist products that are the outputs of your project. These products can be either created, procured or a mixture of the two.

    The suppliers can be internal, external or a mixture of both internal and external.

    Project Manager – The Project Manager, is responsible for the day-2-day management of the project within the agreed tolerances defined by the Project Board (Primarily the Executive). The Project Manager undertakes most of the actual project work in relation to the Management Products or activities (there is a saying – if it looks like work, then the Project Manager does it)

    Team Manager(s) – Can be referred to as Team Leaders, Workstream Leads and can also be known as Project Managers if they are on the supplier side, In this case it is important to remember there can be only one Project Manager with the delegated accountability for the project. The Team Manager role typically manages the teams who create or procure the specialist products that will form the outputs of the project. Dependent upon the project type they could be bricklayers, electricians, IT Developers, Business Process Analysts or any other number of specialist skills. This separation of management and specialist is a key reason for the success of Prince2 as a methodology and also remember they can be internal, external or a mix of the two

Manage by Exception – Management by Exception within Prince2 uses clearly defined, measurable and agreed tolerances to determine if something is wrong. The definition of a tolerance is

"The permissible deviation above and below a plan's target for time and cost without escalating the deviation to the next level of management"

There may also be tolerance levels for quality, scope, benefit and risk. Tolerance is applied at project, stage and team levels

This clear understanding of the permissible tolerances within the project allows the Project manager to understand fully if something is in exception or is forecasted to become an exception. These tolerances are set by the Management Layer above, and this is where the level of authority that is being delegated allows the Project manager to manage the project on a day-2-day basis

In essence Prince2 has no Red, Amber or Green status, as used by most organisations as part of the reporting model. However, it could be easily built into the project. For example

Green level tolerance – could be + / – 2% of Time or Cost
Amber level tolerance – could be + / – 2 to 5% of Time or Cost
Red Level tolerance – could be anything + / – 5% of Time or Cost

Prince2 reports always include information ins relation to identified major issues and risks that the Project Board need to be aware of, this allows the Project Board to understand to understand the ongoing risks associated with the project, this ensures they are up to date in relation to items that could cause the project to go into exception

Manage by Stages – The principle of Manage by Stages, the principle is embedded within the Progress Theme, the Stage Boundary at the end of the Management Stage, which also support the Directing a Project process by ensuring the Project Board maintain control over the project. The stages occur as control points between stages apart from the final stage.

The project progress is assessed by the Project Board, they are reviewing
- The progress and success of the current stage
- Approving its closure
- Approving the next stage
- That they accept the ongoing risks associated with the project

The Project Board will review the Business Case and the Benefits Management Approach to ensure the project remains viable, desirable and achievable supporting the principle of Continued Business Justification

The Business Case and the Benefits Management Approach are 2 of the most important documents within a Prince2 Project and are often through of as the main drivers of the project

The Manage by Stages principle is also linked to the Plans Theme, in Prince2 the assumption (and reality) is that it is not possible to plan a project in detail at the beginning of the project, especially if it is longer than 3-6 months, although this in reality is only a guide and the reality is that it depends upon the uniqueness of the individual project, the environment, the product's and the maturity of the organisation. For this reason alone, it makes sense and is a sensible process to split the project into manageable stages allowing the Project Manager to provide the Project Board with high level milestones and plan in detail for the individual stages as they occur, this allows a greater level of control and understanding

Focus on Products – The Prince2 Principle of Focus on Products is a key reason for the success of both Prince2 as a methodology and its projects, the Principle focuses upon the definition and delivery of the products (both Management Products and Specialist Products) and the definition and prioritisation of the quality requirements

Within Prince2, the word product is interchangeable for deliverables or outputs, especially in relation to Specialist Products, it is crucial to the project's success that the outcome of the project in relation to quality if defined and documented in terms of measurable acceptance relating to the final product

This can only be achieved if each of the individual specialist products that go towards making the final product, satisfy their own measurable quality criteria

This is how the Principle of Focus on Products is embedded within the Quality Theme, however it is less than obvious how or why this Principle is embedded within the Plans Theme, this is where Prince2 recommends the use of the Product Based Planning technique support the identification and definition of the Specialist Products, this enables the Project Manager to understand the products to be delivered before making any assumptions about the activities needed to produce them. This method allows the Project Manager and the team involved to think more about the actual products than the process or activities surrounding them, we will cover this technique later in the book

Learn from Experience – One of the most fundamental Principles of Prince2 is the Principle of Learn from Experience, this is learning from previous projects and passing on learning experiences and opportunities (this is both good and bad experiences) to future projects and also supports the Project Manager when planning the future stages of the current project. This is also built into the Quality Theme through the process of Continual Improvement

Tailor to Suit the Project Environment - The Principle of Tailoring to Suit the Project Environment relates to the tailoring of Prince2 to suit the Project based upon is complexity, its importance, the risks associated with both the delivery and achievement of the projects objectives

The main value of Prince2 is its generic nature, being a universal project management methodology that can be applied to any project, organisation or industry, purely because it is intended to be tailored to suit the project

The purpose of this tailoring is to ensure that

- The project management method used is appropriate to the project (e.g. aligning the method with the business processes that may govern and support the project, such as human resources, finance and procurement)
- Project controls are appropriate to the project's scale, complexity, importance, team capability and risk (e.g. the frequency and formality of reports and reviews).

Tailoring requires a proactive approach to be undertaken by the Project Board and the Project Manager, making decisions on how Prince2 will be applied, it is important to remember that effective Project Management requires information (this is not necessarily documents!) and decisions (not necessarily meetings!)

Tailoring is included within the Project Initiation Documentation (PID) ensuring that all those involved in the Project understand how Prince2 has been tailored, how it will be used and how to carry out or complete their responsibilities relating to the Project

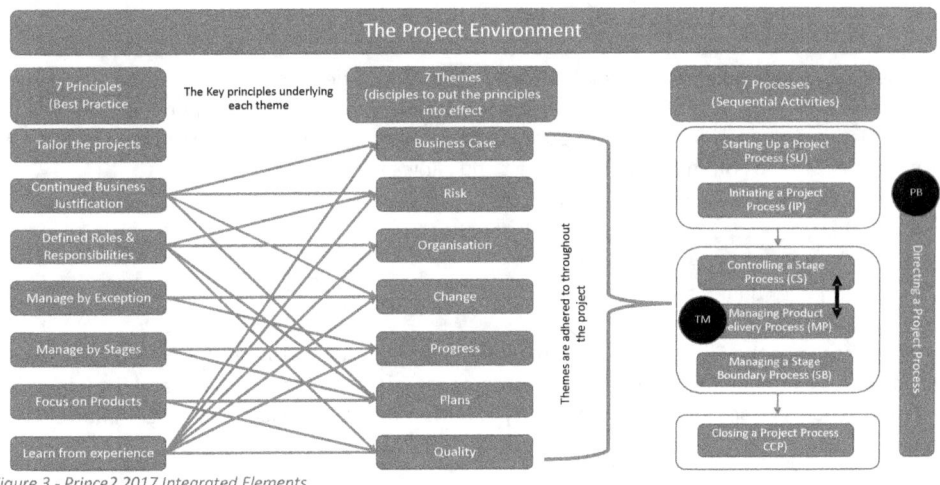

Figure 3 - Prince2 2017 Integrated Elements

Figure 3 (above) shows the links between the Principles and the related Themes, the right-hand side of the diagram shows the Processes within Prince2.

The Starting Up a Project process (SU) and Initiating a Project Process are primarily used to ensure:

- The Project start is controlled,
- The Specialist Products are understood
- The Project Controls are both in place and understood by all of those involved in the Project

These 2 stages are often called Management Stages because the main outputs are Management Products and the remaining stages are called Delivery or Technical Stages

The Controlling a Stage Process (CS) and Managing Product Delivery Process (MP) , are effectively where the Project Manager focuses upon actually managing the Project and is focused upon:

- Managing Team Managers – who are responsible for the creation of the Specialist Products
- Monitoring and Controlling Risks, Issues and Changes
- Reporting Progress
- Liaising with the Project Board for Ad-Hoc Direction as needed

The Managing Stage Boundary Process (SB) occurs (as Prince2 defines it) at or near the end of the current stage, expect the final delivery stage. The Managing a Stage Boundary Process allows the Project Manager to provide the Project Board with sufficient information to allow them to make an informed decision to continue with the Project and allows them to:
- Review the success of the current management stage
- Approve the next stage plan
- Review the updated project plan
- Confirm continued business justification and acceptability of the risks.

The final process is the Closing a Project Process (CP), the Closing a Project Process provides the Project with a fixed point in time, which the acceptance of the Projects Products and the handover of those products to both the User community and the Support and Maintenance Community is completed

The Project Board uses the Directing a Project Process to provide overall control and provides Ad-Hoc direction from the completion of their first official decision, Authorising the Initiation of the Project to their final decision Authorising the Project Closure

3 - How the Processes link together

This chapter focuses upon the 7 Prince2 Processes and how they link together to form the sequential delivery of the projects as indicated below in the diagram

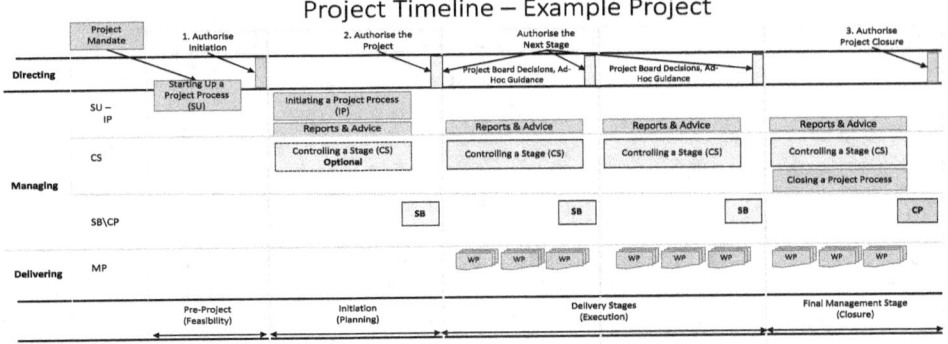

Figure 4 - Prince2 Processes

The 7 Prince2 Processes are:
1. Starting Up a Project Process (SU)
2. Directing a Project Process (DP)
3. Initiating a Project Process (IP)
4. Controlling a Stage Process (CS)
5. Managing Product Delivery Process (MP)
6. Managing a Stage Boundary Process (SB)
7. Closing a Project Process (CP)

Starting up a Project Process (SU) – The Project is triggered by Corporate, Programme or Customer by issuing a Project Mandate. The SU Process is a totally separate process from the Initiation Process and is regarded as Pre-Project, because this process is often more of a feasibility or estimation process because, so little is known about the actual Project, the Specialist Products and the proposed Benefits.

The SU process is aimed at confirming that the Project is to ensure that any pre-requisites for successfully initiating the project are in place and aims to answer the question

Do we have a viable and worthwhile project, the SU process is often a lighter process when compared to the initiating process and aims to do the minimum necessary to obtain the required approvals to initiate the project?

The output of the SU process is the Project Brief, which contains

- The Outline Business Case
- The Project Approach
- The Project Management Team Structure (and any role descriptions)
- The Project Product Description

Directing a Project Process (DP) – This process only officially starts upon the completion of the first decision (Authorisation to Initiate the Project), from that point on the DP Process sits above the project in what is known as the Directing Level and provides direction, guidance and support in the form of Ad-Hoc direction and provides authorisations and approvals at defined control points within the Projects lifecycle through the use of the Managing a Stage Boundary Process (SB) and finally provides authorisation to the close the Project using the Closing a Project Process (CP)

Initiating a Project Process (IP) – The Outline Business Case presents what looks like a viable project that is aligned to Strategic Objectives and the Project Board have given authorisation to initiate the project. The initiation stage is effectively stage 1 of the project.

Within the initiating a Project Process (IP) the contents of the Project Brief are taken and refined into the Project Initiation Documentation (PID) and more documents are added to it, to provide more robust information on the project and its controls. The main outputs of the IP Process are the PID and the Benefits Management Approach

Controlling a Stage Process (CS) – The CS process is effectively where the Project Manager is finally doing what their job spec says, managing the actual project and working in conjunction with the Team Manager(s), who are managing the delivery of the projects Specialist Products

The CS and MP processes are cyclic and dependent upon the Project and the defined number of delivery or technical stages

The CS Process is predominantly undertaken from the perspective of the Project Manager and acts as the link between the Project Manager and the Team Manager

Managing Product Delivery (MP) – The Managing Product Delivery Process (MP) controls the link between the Project Manager and the Team Manager through the agreement of requirements and acceptance (Methods, Criteria, Responsibilities), Execution and Delivery of the Specialist Products through the creation, negotiation, acceptance of Work Packages

The Team Manager's role is to coordinate the work relating to the Work Package, manage the progress through the use of the agreed Team Plan (Optional in Prince2 2017) and reported upon to the Project Manager using the Checkpoint Report

Team Managers can be internal or external to the customers organisation, or can be a mix of internal and external on the same project

Managing a Stage Boundary (SB) – At the end of each Management Stage, the Project Manager will then move into the Managing a Stage Boundary Process (SB), which effectively supports the Directing a Project Process (DP) allowing the Project Board to assert control upon the project by reviewing success (or failure) of the current stage that is coming to close, review the next stage plan and the contents of the Project Initiation Documentation (PID) that have been updated, this will primarily be the Business Case, Project Plan but could be any of the associated documents

The Managing a Stage Process (SB) is conducted "at or near" the end of the current stage on all management stages other than the final stage where it is replaced with the Closing a Project Process (CP)

The main objective of the Managing a Stage Boundary Process is to allow the Project Board to approve the closure of the current stage, approval to proceed to the next stage and confirmation that the project has Continued Business Justification

Closing a Project Process (CP) – At the end of the final delivery stage of the project, the Project Manager focus their attention to the Closing a Project Process (CP). The CP Process is not a stage it replaces the Managing a Stage Boundary process as there are no further delivery stages to be managed.

The CP process is a set of activities that are performed at the end of the final stage to effectively control the projects closure and that the projects outputs (Specialist Products) are handed over to the representatives of the Senior User and those who will maintain and support the products

The CP process can also occur at any point within the Project, and this is the logic behind it being a separate process from the SB Process. In the event the Project is closed early this is termed Premature Closure and can often lead to more work than a controlled CP Process

This is a high-level introduction to the Prince2 2017 Processes, these processes are sequential and are designed to support the achievement of a specific objective, these seven processes provide the activities required to direct, manage and deliver the project successfully

4 - The Project Journey – from start to finish

Project Timeline – Example Project

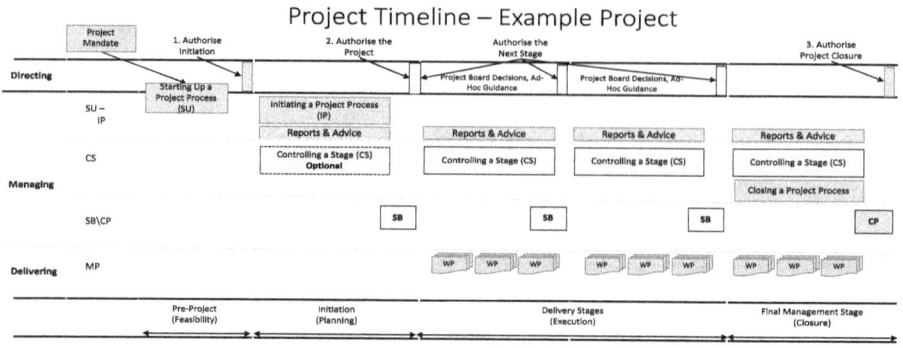

Figure 5 - Prince2 Summary\Line Diagram

The figure above (yes you have seen it before) depicts how the project moves through the 7 Prince2 2017 Processes from the receipt of the Project Mandate to the completion of the Closing a Project Process

This is effectively the simplest way I have found of representing the Prince2 Processes and the Project Lifecycle

Starting Up a Project – let's begin (as any good journey should) at the beginning. The Corporate, Programme or Customer issues a Project Mandate (the trigger) and is given to and appoints the Executive (as a minimum) to the Project Board. The Executive in turn appoints the Project Manager who commences the process of start-up

The major outputs of the Starting Up a Project Process is the Project Brief, which is effectively a project folder that contains:

1. The Outline Business Case
2. The (Draft) Project Product Description
3. The Project Approach
4. The Project Management Team Structure
5. Role Descriptions
6. References to an associated products or documents

The Project Product Description is effectively a high-level specification or design for the Project's final product. It is one of the main drivers or components of the project itself, typically the Project Management Team should have an idea of the measurable that will ensure that the final output of the project will ensure it is it for purpose (effectively meeting the Customers Quality Expectations). If this is not the case, the project will have little or no idea whether the Time, Cost, Quality triangle will be aligned and therefore the project will deliver both Value for Money and a Return on Investment

Initiating a Project – If the Project Board agrees that the project is viable and achievable, they will authorise the project, at this point the project itself is officially commenced and the Directing a Project Process is also officially commenced.

The main output of the Initiating a Project Process (IP) is the Project Initiation Documentation (PID), which is another project folder that contains a set of documents that enable the Project Manager and the Project Board to understand the project and how it will be delivered, and also by whom

The contents of the PID are:
1. The Project Definition
2. The Project Approach
3. The (Detailed) Business Case
4. The Project Management Team Structure
5. Quality Management Approach
6. Change Control Approach
7. Risk Management Approach
8. Communication Management Approach
9. Project Plan
10. Project Controls
11. Tailoring of Prince2

The Project Brief is the initial source of information and is updated and refined as part of the IP process

The Project Plan is an important document in its own right and the creation of this allows the refinement of the estimates and provides a clearer understanding of the specialist products that will be created by the project, which in turn allows further refinement of the Business Case

The IP process also creates the products that will define how the project is managed on a day-2-day basis in the form of a set of approach documents, these are:

- **Quality management approach** - Describes the quality techniques and standards to be applied, and the responsibilities for achieving the required quality levels. Where the project is subject to the commissioning organization's quality management policies/strategies, the PID should make reference to them rather than duplicate them. Where the project is not subject to the commissioning organization's quality management policies/strategies, appropriate strategies/approaches should be documented
- **Change control approach** - Describes how and by whom the project's products will be controlled and protected. Where the project is subject to the commissioning organization's change control policies/strategies, the PID should make reference to them rather than duplicate them. Where the project is not subject to the commissioning organization's change control policies/strategies, appropriate strategies/ approaches should be documented
- **Risk management approach** - Describes the specific risk management techniques and standards to be applied, and the responsibilities for achieving an effective risk management procedure. Where the project is subject to the commissioning organization's risk management policies/strategies, the PID should refer to rather than duplicate them. Where

the project is not subject to the commissioning organization's risk management policies/strategies, appropriate strategies/approaches should be documented

- **Communication management approach** - Defines the parties interested in the project and the means and frequency of communication between them and the project. Where the project is subject to the commissioning organization's communication management policies/strategies, the PID should make reference to them rather than duplicate them. Where the project is not subject to the commissioning organization's communication management policies/strategies, appropriate strategies/approaches should be documented

The IP Process also creates the Benefits Management Approach (the final of the 5 approach documents), however this document is separate from the PID in that it is the only document that remains active or open post project, the Benefits Management Approach documents and defines the:

- The benefits that will be measured post project
- Who is accountable for the benefits?
- What management actions are required in order to ensure the outcomes are achieved
- When the benefits will be measured and against what baselines
- How the benefits will be measured against those baselines
- What specialist resources or tools will be required to measure the benefits

In the scenario where a project is part of a programme, the Benefits Management Approach may be part of the Programmes Benefit Realization Plan and therefore executed at Programme level.

These products are the main decision enabler and driver for the Project Board to make an informed decision as part of the Directing a Project Process when requested by the Project Manager to Authorise the Project

Provided the Business Case is still viable, the Project Board will Authorise the Project (the naming convention here is a little confusing given the project has already effectively been authorised as part of the SU Process), This authorisation allows the work to be commenced on the Specialist Products

Ideally, the Project Board will authorise both the Project and Stage Plan for the next stage at the same time, however (and this is important) this is not necessarily the case, Prince2 allows for the PID and Benefits Management Approach to be approved and therefore the Project to authorised separately from the Next Stage Plan and in some cases, this is a more common-sense approach to be taken

Controlling a Stage and Managing Product Delivery – The first thing the Project Manager needs to do now that they have been given Authorisation to the Deliver the Project is think about the Work Packages associated with this stage and negotiate their delivery with the associated Team Manager(s) through the creation of the Work Package

Work Packages are unique to the individual project in their number and scheduling, there may be multiple Work Packages that can commence together or commence in a defined sequence given the identified dependencies, more typically they will be a mixture of the two.

Typically Work Packages will be undertaken by Suppliers (Given Prince2 assumes all projects are undertaken in a Customer\Supplier environment). These suppliers can be external or internal or a mixture of the two. If the suppliers are external they are assumed to have their own commercial justification for undertaking the project in the form of a Business Case

Once the Project Manager and the Team Manager have agreed the Work Package, the Team Manager is Authorised to Deliver the Work Package by the Project Manager and Executes the Delivery.

The Team manager will now create a Team Plan (optional) to allow the tracking of the Work Package progress and included within this plan will be the details of the reporting requirements. This reporting is in the form of the Checkpoint Report

The Project Manager will us this information when compiling the Highlight Report for the Project Board

** Note the Highlight Report and the Checkpoint Report are the only 2-time driven reports in Prince2 2017, all others are Event Driven Reports **

Another component of the CS Process is to liaise with the Project Board and request Ad-hoc advice and guidance, for example in relation to project risks, or advice in relation to possible issues

Managing a Stage Boundary Process (SB) – In the Pricne2 2017 Manual, it uses the term at or near the end of the current stage, the Project Manager should plan the upcoming stage, this statement assumes there are further delivery stages.

At this point the Project Manager will commence the Managing a Stage Boundary Process (SB), and the main purpose of the SB Process is to enable the Project Manager to provide the Project Board with sufficient information to:
- Review the success of the current stage (the stage coming to an end)
- Approve the next stage (through the information contained within the stage plan)
- Review the updated Project Plan
- Confirm the Continued Business Justification and that they accept the risks associated with proceeding

The Project Manager will update the contents of the PID as applicable, but the main documents to be updated are the Business Case in relation to the any revisions for Time and Cost, the Benefits Management Approach in the event benefits can be realised through the delivery of the projects outputs. This information will also be included within the End Stage Report relating to the overall progress of the project

The approval to close the current stage and approval to commence the next stage are undertaken within the Directing a Project Process, upon notification from the Project Board, the Project Manager will commence the CS Process again and negotiate Work Packages, Produce Highlight Reports and request Ad-Hoc Direction as needed.

These processes of Controlling as Stage Process, Managing a Stage Boundary Process and Authority to Proceed to the next stage are cycles that continue until the project reaches the final delivery stage, whereby the Managing a Stage Boundary Process is replaced with the Closing a Project Process

Closing a Project Process – As the final delivery stage comes towards the end, the Project Manager will switch their attention towards the Closing a Project process (CP), the purpose of the closing a project process is to provide a fixed point at which acceptance of the project's product is confirmed, and to recognize that objectives set out in the original PID have been achieved (or approved changes to the objectives have been achieved), or that the project has nothing more to contribute.

The Project Manager will produce the End Project Report, based upon the information contained within the baselined PID, and the journey the project took taking into account changes, risks, issues that occurred during the projects lifecycle and how they impacted the projects objectives of Time, Cost, Scope, Quality, Risks and Benefits.

This report represents the official close of the project, which should be a clearly defined point where everyone involved with the project understands that the projects Specialist Products have been completed and handed over to both the users and the operations\maintenance teams who will support them. The projects Specialist Products have now switched from Project to BAU\Live\Ongoing maintenance environment and the project team is disbanded

The only piece of the project that officially continues is the Benefits Management Approach that is used by the Senior User who is held accountable for the benefits that were used as part of the approval process for the projects justification

Exception Procedure – In the event the Project forecasts to exceed a tolerance, and to be clear in this scenario the word forecast means that is a known fact that we will exceed the agreed tolerance defined by the Project Board. For example, the project has an agreed cost of $315,000 to complete stage 4, the forecasted costs to deliver the stage is $350,000 which is effectively beyond the stage tolerance for costs which is +\- 10% - effectively $346,500. At this point it is known that we will exceed the tolerance and need to escalate this to the Project Board via an Exception Report

This could also happen because of a major issue, risk which would be handled within the risk or change theme, or simply because the progress of the project requires reviewing

An exception like this is relatively minor and probably will not threaten the overall project in relation to the costs or effect the overall Business Case and the project justification, however if you had this scenario where the increase in funding required was estimated to be in the region $76,500 a 25% increase, this would be "a forecast to exceed the tolerance of both the stage and the project" in this scenario the Business Case may no longer be viable, in this scenario the project board supported by Corporate, Programme or Customer will (most likely) recommend the premature closure of the project unless a major reduction in scope can be agreed whereby the issue causing the forecasted additional funds is removed

It is technically possible to have a premature close at any of the stage boundaries and the Project Board may reject the stage plan and refuse to authorise the next stage because of an external influence from Corporate, Programme or Customer, or a risk has materialised that makes the project no longer viable

5 - The 7 Themes

The 7 Prince2 2017 Themes describe the management actions that must be undertaken by the Project Management Team and continually addressed throughout the lifecycle of the project. This is another strength of Prince2, the integration of the themes, each of the themes has been very carefully designed and matured through lessons to integrate and link together

The Themes address the chronological flow of the project, and the actions that relate to each theme

The Prince2 2017 Themes are

Business Case Theme	How an idea is developed into a viable investment proposition How project management maintains its focus on the organisations objectives throughout a project
Organization Theme	How work is allocated to managers with clear responsibilities How the roles and responsibilities within a Prince2 project team work together efficiently
Quality	How the project management team ensure the requirements are delivered
Plans Theme	How plans are developed using Prince2 techniques How plans are the focus for communications and control throughout the project
Risk Theme	How Project management handles uncertainties in its plans and the environment
Change Theme	How project management assesses and acts upon the need to change, either as a result of changes to requirements or to issues that arise during the project
Progress Theme	How to decide whether to approve a plan How to monitor progress, and what to do when things don't go according to plan

Figure 6 - Prince2 2017 Themes

Business Case Theme – The Outline Business Case is developed during the Starting up a Project Process (SU) or Start-Up Stage and is derived from the Project Mandate (remember – that the SU process is pre-project\feasibility work) and is used as part of the Project Brief to obtain Authorisation to Initiate the project

The Detailed Business Case is then created within the Initiation Stage and the estimates in relation to Time, Cost, Scope, Benefits are refined. The Business Case is then reviewed at each Stage Boundary and also as part of the Risk\Change management process where any risks\issues\changes are reviewed against their possible impact against the projects objectives of Time, Cost, Quality, Scope, Benefits and Risk

It is worth noting that there can be different types of Business Case dependent upon the justification or motivation to undertake the project, whilst most of the motivation is financially drive (make money or save money), however there can also be projects where the justification or motivation is not financial, mandatory or not for profit Business Cases (Compliance, Legislative alignment for example) where the motivation is to avoid a fine or penalty or to avoid reputational damage

Prince2 is very clear that there is no project without an approved Business Case (of some sort, the format can vary dependent upon the organisation)

Typically, the contents of a Business Case would include:

- **Executive Summary** - Highlights the key points in the business case, which should include important benefits and the return on investment

- **Reasons\Justification** - Defines the reasons for undertaking the project and explains how the project will enable the achievement of corporate, programme management or customer strategies and objectives

- **Business Options** - Analysis and reasoned recommendation for the base business options of
  - Do nothing,
  - Do the minimum
  - Do something.

  'Do nothing' should always be the starting option to act as the basis for quantifying the other options. The difference between 'do nothing' and 'do the minimum' or 'do something' is the benefit that the investment will buy

  The analysis of each option provides the project board and the project's stakeholders with sufficient information to judge which option presents the best value for the organization. It provides the answer to the question: for this level of investment, are the anticipated benefits more desirable, viable and achievable than the other options available?

  The business case for the chosen option should be continually assessed for desirability, viability and achievability as any new risks and/or changes may make one of the other options more justifiable

- **Expected Benefits** - These result from the desired outcomes to be achieved through the use of the project outputs. The benefits are expressed in measurable terms against the situation as it exists prior to the project. Benefits should be both qualitative and quantitative

  They should be aligned with corporate, programme management or customer benefits. Tolerances should be set for each benefit and for the aggregated benefit. Any benefits realization requirements should be stated

  The quantification of benefits enables benefits tolerances to be set (e.g. a 10-15 per cent increase in sales) and the measurability of the benefits ensures that they can be proven. If the project includes benefits that cannot be proven, then it is impossible to judge whether the project:
  - has been a success
  - has provided value for money
  - should be (or have been) initiated

  There are many ways to verify the expected benefits. For example, sensitivity analysis can be used to determine whether the business case is heavily dependent on a specific benefit. If it is, this may affect project planning, monitoring and control activities, and risk management, as steps would need to be taken to protect that specific benefit

- **Expected Dis-benefits** - The impact of one or more outcomes of the project might be perceived as negative by one or more stakeholders. Dis-benefits are actual consequences of an activity whereas, by definition, a risk is uncertain and may never materialize. For example, a decision to merge two elements of an organization onto a new site may have benefits (e.g. better joint working), costs (e.g. expanding one of the two sites) and dis-benefits (e.g. drop in productivity during the merger). Dis-benefits need to be valued and incorporated into the investment appraisal

- **Timescale** - The period over which the project will run (a summary of the project plan) and the period over which the benefits will be realized. This information is subsequently used to help timing decisions when planning (project plan, stage plan and benefits management approach)

- **Costs** - A summary of the project costs (taken from the project plan), the ongoing operations and maintenance costs and their funding arrangements

- **Investment Appraisal** - Compares the aggregated benefits and dis-benefits with the project costs (extracted from the project plan) and ongoing incremental operations and maintenance costs. The analysis may use techniques such as cash-flow statement, return on investment, net present value, internal rate of return and payback period. The objective is to be able to define the value of a project as an investment

  The investment appraisal should address how the project will be funded

- Major risks Gives a summary of the key risks associated with the project, together with the likely impact and plans should they occur

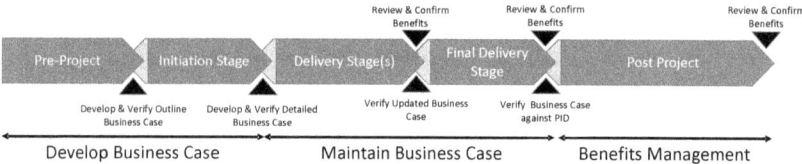

Figure 7 - Business Case

Benefits Management Approach – The Benefits Management Approach defines the management actions that will be put in place to ensure that the projects outcomes are achieved and to confirm that the projects benefits are realised

In the scenario where the project is part of a programme, the Benefits Management Approach may be part of the Programme Benefits Realisation Plan and the benefit management executed\managed at the programme level

The Benefits Management Approach is created as part of the refine the Business Case process during the Initiation Stage, the two documents are linked together and are aligned through the lifecycle of the project

The Benefits Management Approach will typically include:

- The scope of the benefits management approach covering what benefits are to be managed and measured
- Who is accountable for the expected benefits?
- What management actions are required in order to ensure that the project's outcomes are achieved
- How to measure achievement of expected benefits, and when they can be measured
- What resources are needed
- Baseline measures from which the improvements will be calculated
- How the performance of the project's product will be reviewed

Within Prince2 2017, it is assumed that the Senior User(s) (there can be more than one Senior User within a Prince2 2017 project) will be responsible for the provision of the benefits, this is based upon the perception or understanding that as the Senior User(s) will be held accountable for the benefits post project.

The Benefits Management Approach is a key document that enables the Project Board to make a fully informed decision when being asked to Authorise the Project before any major spend or resources are committed, the Benefits Approach also highlights any benefits that will be delivered incrementally (during the projects lifecycle)

The Benefits Management Approach is handed over to Corporate, Programme or Customer as part of the Closing a Project Process as the project team will be disbanded.

Post project benefit reviews will also review the performance of the projects products in operational use and identify whether there have been an adverse effects (beneficial or adverse) that may provide lessons for other projects or improve the maturity of the project processes

Within a Prince2 2017, the Executive is responsible for ensuring the benefits reviews are planned, executed. For projects that are part of Programme environment, the projects benefit management approach may be produced and executed by the programme, as the programme will have roles to coordinate the realisation of the benefits of the projects contained within the programme

Outputs, Outcomes and Benefits – Within Prince2 2017, the specialist products that are delivered are described as the outputs. These outputs in their most simplistic analogy are the products that would not exist if your project did not exist.

These outputs enable the change within the organisation, this can be in many forms for example:
- Business Process Change
- Process enhancement
- Organisational Change
- New products available to sell

It is this change that when used by the user community, enables the realisation of the benefits

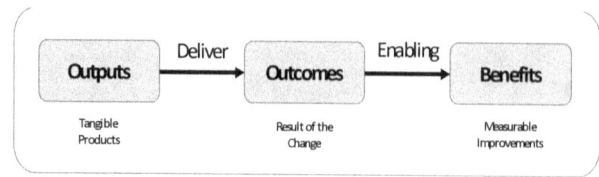

Figure 8 - Outputs, Outcomes & Benefits

In the diagram above, the simple way to remember is
- **Outputs** deliver
  - **Outcomes** enabling
    - **Benefits** to be realised

It is therefore crucial to the project's success that these Outputs are clearly understood, documented and monitored during the projects lifecycle, this monitoring of the Business Case and the Benefits Management Approach directly supports the Principle of Continued Business Justification

Organisation Theme – The Organisation Theme primarily answers the following questions:
- Who is accountable
- Who is responsible

In essence, one of the key drivers to a success project is the establishment of an effective project management team structure and approach to communication, this should be defined at the beginning of the project, and maintained during the projects lifecycle

Within a Prince2 2017 project as we have already discussed, there are three primary interests or roles that must be fulfilled. Whilst Corporate, Programme or Customer act as the sponsors of the project and are the "initiators" through the Project Mandate, it is the Project Board who sits under them who have overall direction and management of the project within the agreed constraints set out by Corporate, Programme of Customer. The Project Board is accountable for the success of the Project

The Project Board may be made up of separate people covering the three roles, or there may be groups of members, for example there could be multiple Senior Users and an Internal and External Senior Supplier on the same Project Board, however within a Prince2 project there can be only 1 Executive with the ultimate decision making ability.

The 3 project interests represented upon the Project Board are:

The Executive - The Executive has ultimate accountability for the project, supported by the Senior User(s) and the Senior Supplier(s) and is the key decision maker, a Prince2 2017 Project Board is not a democracy, the Executive is the final authority and decision maker.

The Executives role is also to ensure the project is fully focused during its lifecycle upon achieving its objectives and that the product (the output) enables the achievement of the forecasted benefits.

The Executive supported by the Project Manager who has day-2-day authority to run the project, ensures that the project is value for money ensuring that the project is delivered using a cost conscious approach – the best way to explain this, if the project was funded by you, would you pay for it. This is effectively the same way the Executive looks at the project balancing the demands of the business, user(s) and suppliers(s)

The Executive is appointed by Corporate, Programme or Customer during the Starting Up a Project Process (Pre-Project) and the role is as we stated above a single individual ensuring a single point of accountability

The Senior User(s) – the Senior User(s) represent the needs of the user community, those individuals or teams who will use or purchase the projects products (outputs), including the operations and maintenance teams. The Senior User(s) is also responsible for ensuring that project product (output) meets the needs of the users within the constraints agreed within the Business Case in relation to Quality, Functionality and Ease of Use

The senior user role commits user resources and monitors products against requirements. For the sake of effectiveness the role should not be split between too many people.

The senior user(s) specifies the benefits and is held to account by demonstrating to corporate, programme management or the customer that the forecasted benefits that were the basis of project approval are in fact realized. This is likely to involve a commitment beyond the end of the project's life.

The Senior Supplier(s) – The Senior User(s) represents the supplier interests, effectively representing the specialist teams or individuals who will create, build or procure the project's product (output), it is not unusual to have more than one supplier or suppliers to change during the lifecycle of complicated or long projects

The Senior Supplier(s) commit the supplier resources required by the project and is accountable for the quality and integrity of the projects products, the Senior Supplier(s) are also responsible for ensuring that proposals to deliver the projects products are feasible and realistic

In most projects, the Senior Supplier(s) will represent the interests of those who will maintain the products after the project product is handed over, for example: IT Operations, Engineering or Facilities

The Project Manager reports to the Project Board, the Project Manager creates the vast majority of the Management Products within the project and is responsible for the day-2-day control of the project. The Project Manager will normally come from the organization sponsoring or hosting the project, however they could also come from the external supplier depending upon the relationship with the customer and the type of project

The Team Manager reports to the Project Manager, and in turn manages the Team Members who undertake the specialist work, these specialists could be brick layers, electricians, web developers, engineers. This is totally dependent upon the project and is another benefit of Prince2 2017, management and specialist work is separated allowing the Project Manager to focus upon the project and its control, and allowing the specialists to undertake the creation of the products. Prince2 2017 does not describe the methods to manage or control the Team Managers or Members as it makes a clear assumption that the supplier will have internal processes that will be followed, so they are effectively operating outside of Prince2 2017

The following roles are classified as option roles within Prince2 2017, this effectively means they can be delegated to an individual or a group of individuals, however if they are not delegated, the functions are still carried by the respective individual

There are primarily 3 additional roles that can be delegates within a Prince2 2017 Project

Project Assurance – **The** project board is responsible, via its project assurance role, for monitoring all aspects of the project's performance and products independently of the project manager.

Project board members are responsible for the aspects of the project assurance role aligned with their respective areas of concern (Business Assurance, User Assurance or Supplier Assurance). If they have sufficient time available, and the appropriate level of skills and knowledge, they may conduct their own project assurance tasks; otherwise they may appoint separate individuals to perform these.

The project board may also make use of other members of the corporate, programme management or customer organization to take on specific project assurance roles, such as appointing the corporate quality manager to monitor the quality aspects of the project.

Project board members are accountable for the project assurance actions aligned with their area of interest, even if they delegate these to separate individuals, they cannot delegate the accountability

Project assurance is not just an independent check, however. Personnel involved in project assurance are also responsible for supporting the project manager, by giving advice and guidance on issues such as the use of corporate standards or the correct personnel to be involved in different aspects of the project (e.g. quality inspections or reviews)

When project assurance tasks are shared between project board members and other individuals, it is important to clarify each person's responsibilities. Anyone appointed to a project assurance role reports to the project board member overseeing the relevant area of interest, and must be independent of the project manager

The project board should not assign any project assurance roles to the project manager or project support

As part of its function to monitor all aspects of the project's performance and products independently of the project manager, project assurance should be involved in all the PRINCE2 processes during the full lifecycle of the project.

The Project Manager cannot be assigned Project Assurance responsibilities within a Prince2 2017 project

Project Support - Project support is the responsibility of the project manager. As with Project Assurance, the Project Manager can delegate some of this work to a Project Support role, this may include providing administrative services or advice and guidance on the use of project management tools.

It could also provide specialist functions to a project such as planning or risk management. In most organizations, the role of Project Support is undertaken by Junior Project Manager and provide support to the Project Manager by undertaking tasks such as Risk Management, Change Management, Financial Support

The role of project support is not optional, but the allocation of a separate individual or group to carry out the required tasks is. The role defaults to the project manager if it is not otherwise allocated.

Changer Authority – During the initiation Process, it is crucial that the decision on who is permitted to authorize requests for change od off specifications is understood and clearly documented, even (especially) if the answer is only the Project Board.

It is the project board's responsibility to agree to each potential change before it is implemented. In a project where few changes are envisaged, it may be reasonable to leave this authority in the hands of the project board. But projects may be in a dynamic environment, where there are likely to be, for example, many requests to change the initial agreed scope of the project. Technical knowledge may also be needed to evaluate potential changes.

The Project Board needs to decide before the project leaves the Initiation Process if the Change Authority role will be delegated to a group or a individual, If it delegates some of this authority to approve or reject requests for change or off-specifications, this delegation must be documented and contained within the appropriate role descriptions

The Project Manager and Project Assurance can be granted delegated authority for Changes

Roles Vs People – Within a Prince2 2017 Project the structure is known as the Project Management Structure and is represented below

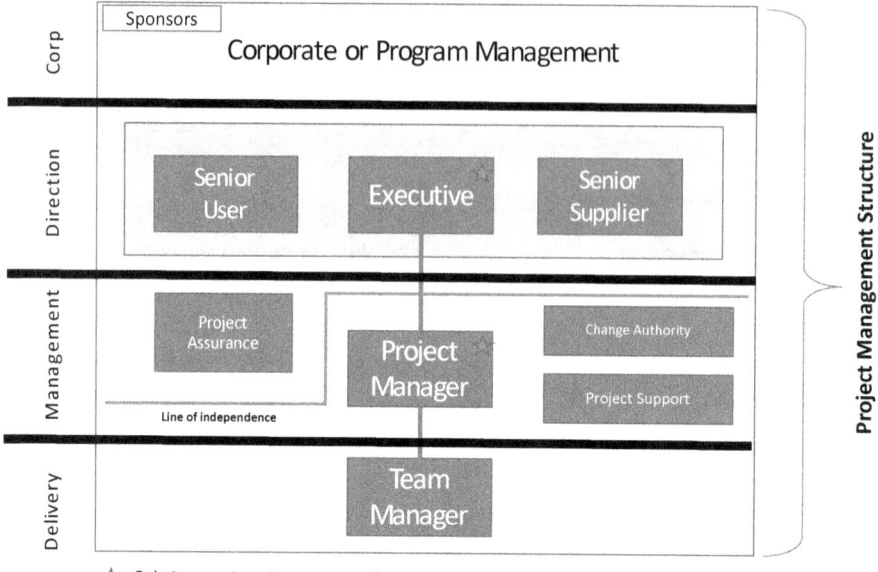

Only 1 per project, 1 person per role

Figure 9 - Project Management Structure

The diagram above is a representation, the roles listed are roles and not necessarily people. This effectively means that the Project Management Structure can be tailored (and should be) to the project. Effectively one role can be shared by more than one person or one person can act as a single role, however it is important that each role is undertaken

It is also key to understand that certain roles are absolutely crucial to the overall success of the project and only one person and only one role can exist within the project, I always remember the line from Highlander – "there care be only one" and this is true of the Executive and Project Manager roles

In the most simplistic of Pricne2 2017 projects, this is effectively the minimum needed to carry out all roles, with the Executive taking on the responsibilities of the Project Board and undertaking all of their own assurance (everything above the line of independence) and the Project Manager undertaking all other roles including those of the Team Manager by engaging with the Team Members and also completing all of their own support

The Project Board will appoint people into the required roles based upon the projects need or the skills required, this is true especially for Project Assurance if the Project Board does not have the required skills or time needed to support the project on a day-2-day basis.

The Project Manager may appoint people as Team Managers or they may be appointed by the Senior Supplier (this will be the case in most projects where the supplier is external), this can be done for a number of reasons, for example: ON larger projects where multiple products will be created, if the Project Manager is not a subject matter expert, geographical locations make it difficult for the Project Manager to assume the role of Team Manager.

The Project Board – The Project Board are primarily there to provide the "decision making" and not to act as a conversation\talking shop. The Project Board will provide authorisations\approvals at key points defined within the Project Plan for the Project in the form of Stage Boundary's where they authorise the closure of the current stage and the authorisation to commence the next stage. If the Project Board is too large or has people who are their unnecessarily, this process can be delayed of become time consuming for the Project Manager, which in turn takes them away for from their primary role of managing and controlling the project on a day-2-day basis. The size of the Project Board needs to be effective and the three primary roles covered, but not filled with unnecessary members who could meddle or intrude in their justification to be there. This is a balancing act whereby the justification for the right people and the justification for those not needed to be at a lower level can take time and cause delays within the Initiation Process

Prince2 2017 suggests the Project Board should be kept as small as possible

Project Board Meetings – How often is too often? – Prince2 2017 clearly states that meeting the Project Board is only needed as part of the Stage Boundary Process, however as we all know that the Project Board and the Project Manager will meet within the stage, however this goes directly against the Principle of Manage by Exception!

There are however a number of valid and justified reasons why the Project Board and the Project Manager should meet within the stage, and it could also be argued that this is a more effective use of both the Project Board and the Project Managers time, for example:

- As part of Ad-Hoc guidance, if there are genuine decisions being made at these meetings in relation to risks\issues and general guidance from the Project Board to support the project and maintaining its forward momentum

These meetings could be cancelled if not required, and therefore it could be argued that this is a more effective use of the Ad-Hoc direction, especially if the Project Board are carrying out the roles of Project Assurance

Again, this is a balancing act with ensuring the Project Board have sufficient information to garner their trust in both the process and the Project Manager, the use of Highlight Reports is crucial to this process

Stakeholders – The Prince2 2017 definition of a stakeholder is:
"Any individual, group or organization that can affect, be affected by, or perceive itself to be affected by, an initiative (i.e. a programme, project, activity or risk)"

Which can be perceived as anyone who has a positive or negative view upon the project, this also obviously includes Corporate, Programme or Customer, all of the Project Management Team members, the Team Manager(s) and Team Members (who are often overlooked)

This can also include people who are external to the Project, and possibly even external to the organization hosting the project dependent upon the type of project

It is crucial to identify the stakeholders and analyze them to understand their levels of influence\impact upon the project

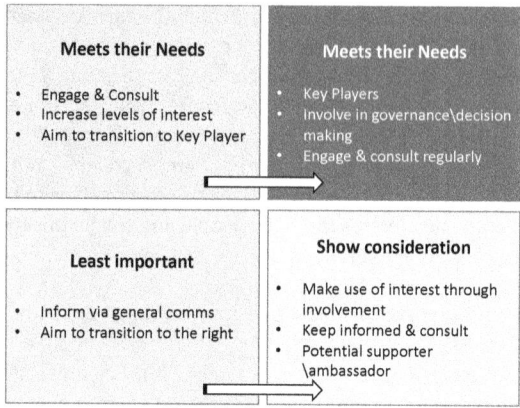

Figure 10 - Stakeholder Map

Once the stakeholders are identified, now we need to understand how to communicate with them effectively, this should be a 2-way process allowing them to communicate with the Project Manager as well. This is documented within the Communication Management Approach

The Communication Management Approach contains a description of the means (email, report, meeting) and frequency of communication to parties both internal and external to the project.

The primary goal of the Communication Management Approach is ensure that all identified stakeholders have a clear engagement process that is both controlled and bi-directional

Where the project is part of a program, the Communication Management Approach should align with the programs approach to Stakeholder Communication and Engagement.

Quality Theme – The aim of the Quality Theme is to define and implement the means by which the project will verify that products are fit for purpose, as early as possible the Project Manager needs to get an understanding of the customers quality expectations. The risk of doing this so early in the project is that these terms may be vague and unclear

The customers quality expectation are primarily their view of what "fit for purpose" looks like, at the early stages of the project these expectations are translated into the Project Product Description and should include some form of acceptance criteria for the project

The easiest way to describe the Project Product Description is:

- A high level document that provides an overview of
  - What must be delivered to obtain acceptance from the Senior User and Executive
  - Confirm the projects scope and requirements
  - Define what "fit for purpose" looks like in the form of Customers Quality Expectations

- o Define the acceptance criteria, methods of measurement and acceptance responsibilities

If your project is deliver a house, and the customer states Customers Quality Expectations as

- Bigger than our current house
- A large garage
- Lots of bathrooms and storage

This is not sufficient to allow the Project Manager to create any realistic estimate of Time and Cost for the project, the customer should be pushed to provide a more detailed explanation of their expectations

- Minimum of 4 bedrooms
- 2 with Ensuite bathrooms
- 1 family bathroom
- 2 car garage with storage

This allows the Project Manager to understand the project better, their expectations are the same, they have simply been explained in better detail and these can now be turned into measurable acceptance criteria

The Prince2 2017 definition of acceptance criteria is - A prioritized list of criteria that the project product must meet before the customer will accept it (i.e. measurable definitions of the attributes required for the set of products to be acceptable to key stakeholders).

The Draft Project Product Description will be created by the Project Manager during the Start Up stage, to allow the creation of high level estimates for Time and Cost supporting the Outline Business Case, these will be refined during the Initiation Process

During the Initiation Process, the Project Manager will be a technique called Product Based Planning, this process will identify the core products being delivered by the project and (at least) the major individual products that will go make up the projects specialist products (we will go through this technique later in the book as part of the Plans Theme)

The House Product Based Plan would look something like the diagram below

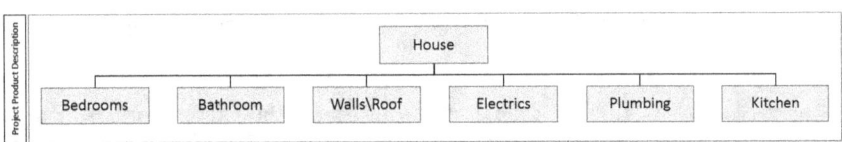

Figure 11 - Product Based Plan

Each of the major specialist products (the Bedrooms, Bathrooms) will have their own Product Descriptions which are in a much lower level of detail than the Project Product Description. These will contain more details upon

- The customers' prioritised requirements
- The acceptance criteria that needs to be met,
- Any tolerances relating to the quality or acceptance criteria
- The quality method – how it will be measured and any specific tools or skills needed
- The quality responsibilities – who will measure and accept the product

This information is then documented into the Quality Management Approach

The Quality Management Approach – describes how quality will be managed within the project, this will include any specific processes, techniques, standard and responsibilities.

The Quality Management Approach is created within the Initiation Process and is one of the 5 approach documents, we have reviewed the Benefits Management Approach and the Communication Management Approach, and will review the Risk and Change Control Approaches in their respective Themes

Once the Quality Management Approach is documented, the Project Manager will open the Quality Register, which is used to summarize all of the quality management activities that are planned and provides information for the end stage reports and end project reports through the provision of information on the activities that are planned and those that have taken place

The Quality Register:

- Issues a unique ID or reference for each quality activity
- Acts as a pointer to the quality records for each product (both specialist and management)
- Acts as a summary of the number and type of quality activities undertaken or to be undertaken

In its most simplistic format the Quality Register is a "diary of quality activities and checks" and lists the activities\checks for each product within each stage. This Management Product overlaps between the Quality Planning undertaken by the Project Manager and the Quality Control that is the responsibility of the Team Manager(s)

The planned checks for the next stage are included or inserted into the Quality Register by the Project Manager whilst they are planning it as part of the Stage Boundary process, then the results are inputted by the Team Manager(s) as part of the Managing Product Delivery process , although if the Project Manager has Project Support, they will normally be charged with the maintenance of the Quality Register

The final piece of the Quality Theme is the Acceptance Records, these records are the final part of Managing Product Delivery and are provided as part of the Quality Review Technique. The product is reviewed against the Product Description and agreed Work Package by a representative of the Senior User(s) and if the product meets the required levels of quality and acceptance criteria it will approved and accepted.

There are circumstances where a product could be delivered and accepted event though it does not fully meet the criteria, but it will be resolved in a patch or later version, this is called accepted with conditions within Prince2 2017

The diagram below shows the Prince2 2017 path to quality linked to the above:

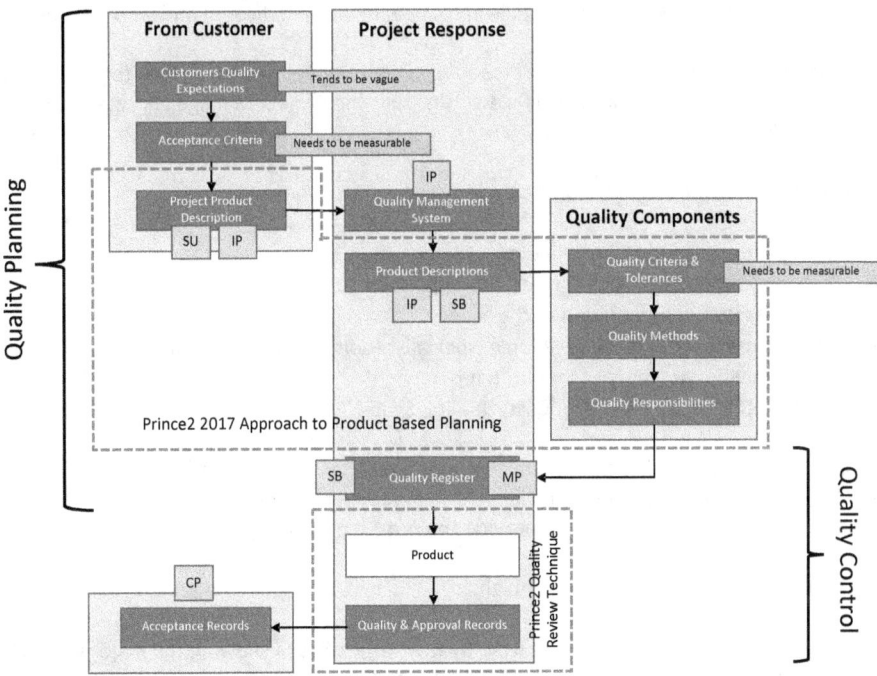

Figure 12 - Prince2 Path to Quality

Quality Assurance – Quality Assurance is function within the host organisation that establishes and maintains the organisations Quality Management Systems (ISO, BSI etc) This role is often thought of as an Internal Audit or Compliance function

It is important to remember that *Quality Assurance is external* to the Project, whilst *Project Assurance is internal* to the project and is part of the Project Management Team.

They both involve some form of independent monitoring, Quality Assurance typically monitors that the project is compliant with organisational standards on behalf of Corporate, Program or Customer, whilst Project Assurance monitors compliance with Prince2 for example that right people are involved, the tailoring of Prince2 is suited to the project, the solution being delivered is acceptable on behalf of the Project Board

Plans Theme – The Pans Theme within Prince2 2017 to facilitate communication and control by defining the means of delivering the products, it answers the
- The where will the products be products
- By whom will they be produced

And direct enables the Project Manager to estimate the Time and Cost

When you mention a Project Plan to most people, their first thought is that or a chart showing the timeline of the projects products being delivered, in Prince2 2017 the Project Plan takes a more comprehensive and flexible view of the plan. The Prince2 2017 Project Plan describes not only the timescales, but also covers what will be delivered, how it will be delivered and who will deliver it.

Poorly planned projects cause wastage of resources, time, money and often lead to products that are produced being unfit for purpose. It is essential that the Project Manage allocates sufficient time for planning to take place

The Plan enables the full Project Team to understand:

- What products need to be delivered
- The risks associated – both threats and opportunities
- Any issues with the definition of the scope
- What resources are needed – People, specialist tools, skills, equipment
- When activities and event "should" happen
- Whether the targets for Time, Cost, Quality, Scope, Benefits and Risks are achievable

The plan provides the baseline against which the progress can be measured and is the basis for the Project Manager to secure support for the project, agreeing the scope (and also what is out of scope) and gaining the commitment to provide the required resources

Within Prince2 2017 there are 3 types of plan,

- Project Plan – the high level plan used by the Project Board showing the major products of the project, when and how they will be delivered and at what cost
- Stage Plan – The detailed plan used by the Project Manager as the basis for control throughout the relevant management stage
- Team Plan – Each could comprise of any number of Work Packages depending upon the products being produced, each of those products requires a detailed plan to track its progress, the Team Plan in Prince2 2017 is optional however

The relationship between Project Lifecycles, Phases and Stages. Project lifecycles are often described in terms of project phases, where the term 'phase' is used as an alternative to 'stage' or 'management stage'.

For example, BS 6079-1:2010 states:

Most projects, irrespective of size and complexity, will naturally move through a series of distinct phases from conception to completion. This applies as much for sequential development (e.g. analyse, design, build, test) as for iterative and agile development. Generally, the early phases comprise investigative work, which determines the work in the later implementation phases.

In BS 6079 Part 1, there is no assumption regarding the use of the words 'phase' or 'stage' with respect to level in the work breakdown structure; for example, a stage is not assumed to be a sub-part of a phase or vice versa.

The final type of plan in Prince2 2017 is the Exception Plan, as reviewed earlier if we are forecasting that we cannot complete a stage within the tolerance agreed, for example time. The Project Board will ask the Project Manager to provide an Exception Plan to replace the current stage plan and show the situation will be recovered (assuming it can)

If we are forecasting to exceed the Project Tolerance, dependent upon the level, if the Business Case still remains valid the Project Board will review with Corporate, Program or Customer and will again ask the Project Manager to create an Exception Plan to recover the overall project

In the event that the Business Case is no longer viable, the Project Board will review the project again with Corporate, Program or Customer as to the continued viability of the project and agree if it should be prematurely closed

In contrast, if the threat is only to a Work Package or Team Plan, this is resolved as a project issue and does not require an Exception Plan (as shown by the dotted lines in Figure 13

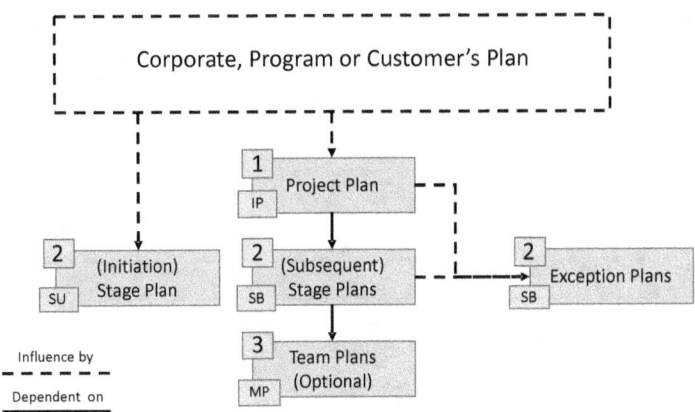

Figure 13 - Prince2 2017 Plans

Management Stages – The Principle of Management by Stages is fundamental to the success and enables the planning of the project around crucial points, these could be decisions, acceptance, key milestones, changes in suppliers or key resources that allow the Project Board to assess:

- Whether the project continues to be justified
- That the previous stage has been completed
- The approval of the next Stage Plan
- The continued acceptance of the risks

Within Prince2 2017, there must be a minimum of 2 stages to be following the Principle of Management by Stages and the Plans Themes, this is even on a simple project to act as a control point between the initiation and the delivery stages. On larger projects the decision upon the number of stages is driven by a number of factors:

- The nature of the products being delivered
- The complexity of the projects
- The governance models to be followed
- The planning horizon – how far ahead can be practically planned
- Alignment to the programme
- The risks associated
- The level of control required by the Project Board

In our diagram below (Figure 14), the example project has

- Start Up Stage – Pre-Project\Feasibility
- Initiation Stage – Planning
- 3 Delivery Stages
- Final Delivery Stage with Closure

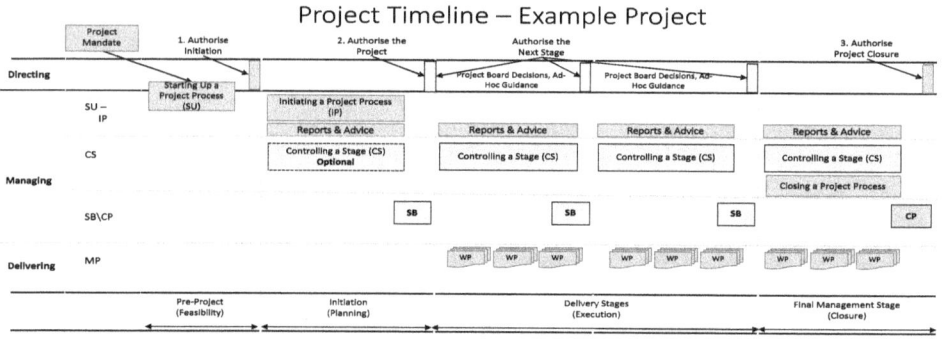

Figure 14 - Example Project

In essence, if any stage is planned to be longer than 3-6 months it would make sense to break it down to enable a more realistic planning horizon.

If there is a major product or major risk point within the project, it again would make sense to make that as a Stage Boundary, this enables the Project Board to have a clear decision point on the continued viability of the project

In periods where the project is classed as low risk, or low complexity, it would make sense to reduce the control points and in essence have a longer Management Stage, adversely it makes sense to have smaller more control points where the project is a complex or risky stage enabling more control points, it may also be more prudent to review the tolerances associated with the stage as well

Within Prince2 2017, Management Stages do no overlap, there can only be one Management Stage, this is to ensure that there is a definitive control point whereby the Project Board have a clear decision and approval to proceed to the next stage

This also enables the progress to be assessed and used to forecast forward for the rest of the project, if stages overlapped there would be confusion and no clear idea of the projects progress and a clear lack of control relating to the Project Board

Project Planning – Project Managers with little Prince2 experience will often jump straight into planning with the creation of the Gantt Chart, this is often done using MS Project, Excel or online planning software.

Prince2 2017 however, regards the plan as previously mentioned as a document that is far more detailed and a Gantt chart simply fails to show that level of detail, for example tolerances and anyone who has viewed a Gantt chart that they have not been involved in the creation of, will quickly realise that they struggle to read and understand the chart as it has been created in isolation

Product Based Planning – The Prince2 approach to planning differs from other methodologies, it is based upon the Principle of Focus on Products and recommends the use of the Product based Planning technique (One of the few techniques Prince2 recommends) to identify the products, dependencies, associations, sequence and allows a more refined estimate for the time and costs

I personally started this way and when I first started out as a Project Manager, I firmly believed this is the way a project was planned. However my first real Programme Manager introduced me to Product Based Planning, Since that introduction I have been a huge fan of the technique and everyone who I have taught and demonstrated it too has said it extremely useful in both planning and also the ability to show the products to the Project Management Team

There are 4 steps within the technique,

1. The first is to document the Project Product Description
2. The second is to create the Product Breakdown Structure
3. The third is to create of the individual product descriptions
4. The final step is to create the Product Flow Diagram (In Prince2 2017 this is an optional step)

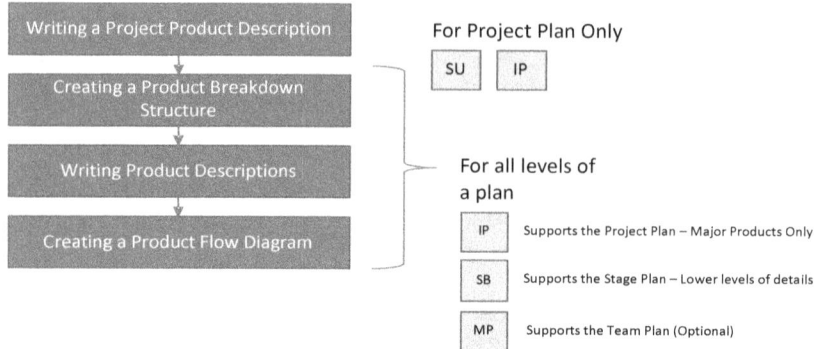

Figure 15 - Defining and Analysing Products

Step 1 - The Project Product Description - The Project Product Description is created in the starting up a project process as part of the initial scoping activity. It may be refined during the initiating a project process when creating the project plan. It is subject to formal change control and should be checked at management stage boundaries (during the managing a stage boundary process) to see if any changes are required. It is used in the closing a project process as part of the verification that the project has delivered what was expected of it and that the acceptance criteria have been met.

Although the senior user is responsible for specifying the project product, in practice the project product description is often written by the project manager in consultation with the senior user and executive. The project product description is included as a component of the project brief and is used to help select the project approach defined within the project brief.

The project product description defines what the customer is expecting the project to deliver and the project approach defines the solution or method to be used by the supplier to create the product, remembering that Prince2 2017 assumes all projects are Customer\Supplier based projects

It is key to try and make sure the Project Product Description as complete as possible as early in the process as possible

Step 2 – The Product Breakdown Structure - This is primarily a visual representation of the projects output and the main components needed to make it or when combined together will make the projects product (see Figure 11)

The best way to produce a Product Breakdown Structure is through the use of workshops or meetings where the project is discussed and the interests of the Business, User and (if possible) the Supplier are represented, when I do this exercise I have access to a room with a whiteboard wall that's 8ft high and 20ft long and use post-its and whiteboard pens, this allows things to be written and moved around based upon the feedback and guidance of the Subject Matter Experts. The risk around these meetings is that they can get out of hand and have to be closely managed and controlled. This often means as the Project Manager or Programme Manager (dependent upon my role within the project) I become more of a facilitator. This process also has another added bonus, in that it helps garner trust from the Project Board and its members, and plays a key role in ensuring that the "golden triangle" for time, cost and quality

The Product Breakdown Structure helps identify the key products, product groups and then allows the focus to drop into the individual products which is essentially step 3

Step 3 – Product Descriptions – During the process of creating the Product Breakdown Structure, it will naturally identify individual products that are required for the project to be a success, and in some instances the sequence of their delivery and dependencies.

It is crucial that as they are identified, as much information is obtained to support the creation of the draft Product Description, the main contents of the Product Description according to Prince2 2017

The Product Descriptions can be defined at any point during the project, however within a Prince2 2017 project they are approved as either updated or new Product Descriptions during the Managing Stage Boundary Process

The final step (which is optional) is the Product Flow Diagram,

Step 4 – The Product Flow Diagram - The Product Flow Diagram shows the products in the order in which they will be delivered, procured or created.

When does all of this happen, the Product Breakdown Structure is created or drawn up during the Starting Up Process, however as discussed at this point it is probably very high level and in some instances will only have product names.

This is then refined during the Initiation Process as part of the overall planning for the project and as such much more detailed Product Descriptions that include detailed quality details

These are then as mentioned already, these are revisited at each Stage Boundary as part of the review process, this could change the entire next stage by adding in new Products or refining Products being delivered

In larger projects where separate team plans are required, it may be that the Team Manager(s) as part of the definition of the Team Plans break the Products into an even lower level of detail

External Products – It is important to understand the term External Products and what they are, Prince2 2017 defines an External Product as "a product that already exists or is being created outside of the project or the scope of the project"

The simple way to think of this is, something your project needs but you are not paying for and have no control over the quality

An example could be if your project requires an export from a HR System and it is a dependency, you have no control over the quality of the data contained within the HR system, it could be delivered on time, but the data contained is not accurate or up to date

External Products are often also registered as risks for these very reasons

Risk Theme – Prince2 2017 projects by their very nature introduce change, which is the introduction of uncertainty. Uncertainty is essentially risk. Projects always include or involve risk. As much as you would like to ignore risks, they must be effectively managed no matter the project or its size

In mature organisations, there will differing levels of Risk Appetite, some organisations may have a high appetite when managing risks and others may have an extremely low appetite, it can also be that it differs within the individual organisation or even to the extent of between individual projects

A Prince2 2017 project understands that risks can be both negative and positive and as such has the definition of Threats and Opportunities

Threats - Uncertain events that would have a negative impact on objectives
Opportunities - Uncertain events that would have a positive impact on objectives

Prince2 2017 has a defined 5 step procedure for the management of risks

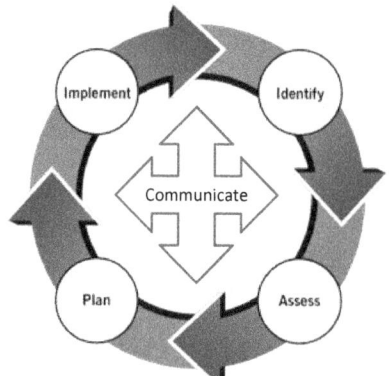

Figure 16 - Risk Management Procedure

Risk Management Procedure - The 5 steps are
1. Identify
2. Assess
3. Plan
4. Implement
5. Communicate

We will review each of the steps individually, you will be surprised at how you manage risks everyday using just common sense, because at the end of the day common sense is the core of being a Project Manager and managing projects

We will use a simple risk that has been raised as part of the process of understanding risk within Prince2 2017 and walk through the 5 step process

Step 1 – Identify – The Identify step is broken into 3 parts
1. Cause – The underlying cause of the risk
2. Event – The event it gives rise to
3. Effect – The effect created

For example, anyone who travels a lot for work, knows they run the risk of arriving late – this is the effect, if your using the train, particularly in London, this is the cause and the event is the train running late. Given this the risk would be explained as

The train from London could be late (Cause) which would cause me to be late (Event) and miss the meeting (Effect)

Which is a much better way of explaining a risk – the same risk could be simply listed as the trains could run late in London, however this gives little or no context to the actual risk or its effects

It is crucial to learn to describe risks in this manner as this helps with Step 2 – Assess

Step 2 – Assess – Now that we understand the risk given its cause m event and effect. The next step is to assess the risk and quantify it

We will try and assess the risk based upon the following:

Probability – The probability of the risk actually occurring
Impact – The impact of the risk upon the objectives of the project – Time, Cost, Scope, Quality, Risk and Benefits

Once the risk has been assessed for the Probability and Impact, we will try and understand the proximity of the risk. This can be quantified in many ways, for example:
- Imminent
- In Stage
- Work Package
- Within project
- External to the Project

The risk we have as an example,

The train from London could be late (Cause) which would cause me to be late (Event) and miss the meeting (Effect)

Within this risk the assessment would be

Probability – The probability of actually be late for the meeting or missing the meeting is high due t the train being late given the regular late departures
Impact – The Impact (or effect) of the risk upon the objective (of being at the meeting on time) upon the objectives is medium (primarily effecting the objective of time)

The proximity, is imminent for this particular risk

Step 3 – Plan – Step 3 – Plan is effectively planning the responses to the risk, having undertaken the assessment of the risk and understanding its probability, impact and proximity. The risk now needs to be assessed in terms of the most effective response to either reduce the probability of the risk occurring, or the impact of the risk it is does occur. Or alternatively a mixture of reducing the probability and impact as some risks it is now possible or achievable to reduce the probability or impact fully

Within Prince2 2017, there are primarily 6 responses to risks
1. Avoid
2. Reduce
3. Transfer
4. Share
5. Accept
6. Prepare Contingency Plans

Avoid – The response Avoid aims to completely remove the risk by taking the probability the risk occurring to zero, in our example risk –
- an option to avoid would be to have the meeting as a conference call is possible or them to come to the office in London
- or to drive to the meeting, avoiding the need to use the train, however this would potentially introduce a secondary risk with the same effect of arriving later for the meeting or missing it altogether

Reduce – This is often the easiest of the risk responses to actually implement and often the most common within projects. This response aims to reduce the probability of the risk occurring or the impact in the event it does occur, but the risk itself is not reduced to zero

What remains of the risk – the residual risk – is reduced, but the risk remains in a lower classification in relation to probability or impact

In the risk identified, getting an earlier train would reduce the probability and impact and is also a cost effective response to the risk, it still leaves the possibility of being late but the probability is reduced greatly and could now be classed as a probability of Low or Very Low

Transfer – This response is aimed at specific types of threats where they can be "transferred to a third party", where some or all of the risk is transferred to a third party, this is typically undertaken using a penalty clause for example

A supplier must deliver a product by a certain date, otherwise the contract includes payment penalties, in this example the majority of the risk is transferred to the supplier, although a small risk remains within the project as it could still be delivered late.

Share – The share response is an option that is different in nature from the transfer response. It seeks multiple parties, typically within a supply chain, to share the risk on a pain/gain share basis. An example would be where a contract is written that a customer is purchasing a large amount of steel and the contract is written that the price is capped at $100 per tonne and if the price rises to $110 it will remain at $100 or if it falls below $90 it will remain.

In the event it falls below $90 or rises above $110, both the supplier and the customer have recourse to renegotiate the contract, this was the risk is shared between both parties

Accept – Under certain scenarios, it make sense to simply accept the risk, if a risk is classed as having a probability of very low or low and impact of very low or low, then it is possible more cost effective to accept the risk rather than spend time and effort undertaking a full assessment and planning a response to reduce it further in terms of probability and impact

Prepare Contingency Plan – This is the classic disaster recovery scenario, it involves having plans in place but taking no action until the risk occurs (or becomes an issue)

The Prepare Contingency Plans is often aligned to the accept option, we accept the risk but will prepare plans in the event it occurs, it can apply equally to all other responses as a secondary plan in the event the residual risk occurs

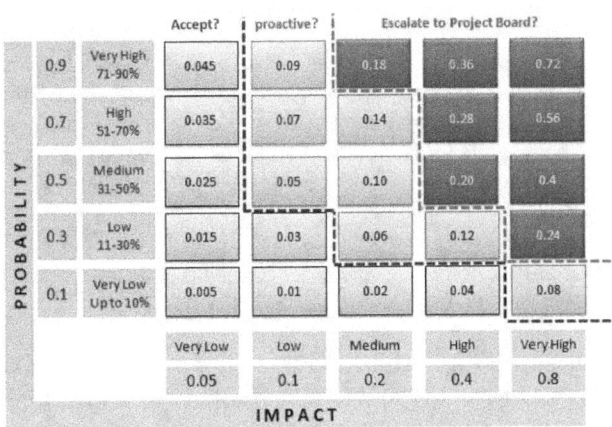

Figure 17 - Summary Risk Profile

As with Threats, Opportunities have responses as well. The three main responses to these are:
1. Exploit
2. Enhance
3. Accept

Exploit – is the opposite of avoid in relation to a threat, with the response Exploit you are taking physical steps to ensure the opportunity actually occurs, ideally at no cost

Enhance – is similar to the Exploit response, however your taking steps to ensure it occurs and actually taking steps to ensure the maximum effect of the opportunity occurs, this can have a cost incurred through the process of enhancing the opportunity

Accept – As with the accept response to a risk, the accept response to an opportunity, effectively means the opportunity is simply not viable or too expensive to actually achieve and therefore the simplest solution is to accept the opportunity, which is a simple way of saying the opportunity is rejected

Once the appropriate responses is understood and agreed, the next step is to Implement the risk response or monitor the risk using early warning indicators

Step 4 – Implement – The responses to the risks need to be actioned and their effectiveness monitored and if required further corrective action undertaken of the selected response does not provide the expected results

As part of this, it is critical to the monitoring that a Risk Owner and Risk Actionee are identified for each risk;

These roles responsible for:

The first role is that of **Risk Owner** – The Risk Owner is responsible for the management, monitoring and control of the risks assigned to them. This can be an individual risk or a number of risks. This includes the implementation of the responses

This should ideally be the person who is best placed and qualified to implement any proactive responses or monitor any identified early warning indicators associated with the risk, and monitor the risk and provide updates or information relating to the risk to the Project Manager. The information provided back to the Project Manager is in relation to the risk and its current status, has it improved, is it worsening or remaining as originally identified – all in relation to the probability and impact

The second role is that or **Risk Actionee** – the Risk Actionee is assigned to carry out the planned response to the relevant risk, they directly support the Risk Owner

The final step is Communicate – Which is not really a step as such, but is in fact carried out both throughout the lifecycle of the project and also the lifecycle of the risk itself.

The communication is carried using the various reports within Prince2 2017

- Checkpoint Reports – between the Team Manager and the Project Manager to communicate upon risks or raise risks relating to Work Packages
- Highlight Reports – From the Project Manager to the Project Board and provides information on existing risks and new risks that have been raised that the Project Board should be informed about
- End Stage Reports – relating to risks that have been raised or closed during the stage
- End Project Reports – relating to Major Risks that were raised or occurred during the projects lifecycle and had an impact upon project objectives
- Lessons Reports – at both stage and end of project, to support lessons to improve both the project and risk management across the organisation
- Exception Reports – if required relating to risks that have become issues

Risk Management Products

The management products relating to the Risk Theme are:

- The Risk Management Approach
- The Risk Register

The Risk Management Approach – as previously discussed, there are 5 management approaches, the Risk Management Approach defines the management approach to Risk within the context of the project and includes the alignment to Corporate, Programme or Customer Risk Management Practices.

It describes the procedures, techniques, standards and scales that will be used, including the responsibilities relating to the management of risks.

Much of the context of the Risk Management Approach will come from the risk context in relation to the project itself, the Project Boards approach to risk and the organisations Risk Management standards, the complexity of the project itself, this forms part of the first step Identify. The identification of the Risk Management processes, procedures and scales.

The second is the Risk Register, which contains all of the information relating to the individual risks and the management actions relating to them. This is a living document that is opened during the Initiation Stage

Probability and Impact Grids (Summary Risk Profiles)

Probability and Impact Grids, which are also known as Summary Risk Profiles are visual representations used to present the number of risks within the project and also aid the Project Manager in assessing the risks in relation to the Probability and Impact as shown below in the diagram

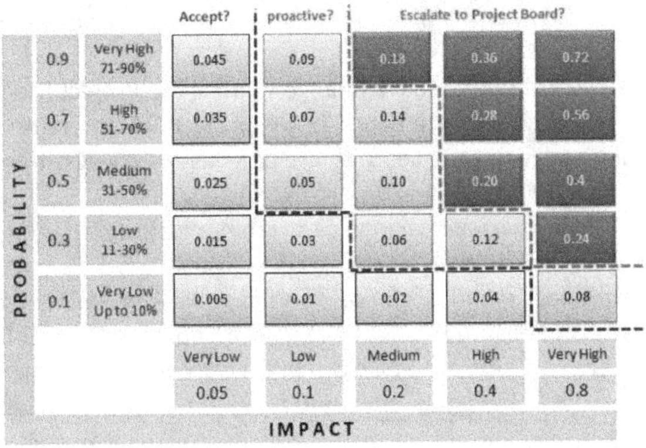

		Accept?	proactive?		Escalate to Project Board?	
0.9	Very High 71-90%	0.045	0.09	0.18	0.36	0.72
0.7	High 51-70%	0.035	0.07	0.14	0.28	0.56
0.5	Medium 31-50%	0.025	0.05	0.10	0.20	0.4
0.3	Low 11-30%	0.015	0.03	0.06	0.12	0.24
0.1	Very Low Up to 10%	0.005	0.01	0.02	0.04	0.08
		Very Low	Low	Medium	High	Very High
		0.05	0.1	0.2	0.4	0.8

PROBABILITY

IMPACT

Figure 18 - Probability & Impact Grid

The grid contains the values that are used to rank\assess the threats and opportunities qualitatively. The scales are measures that can be shown as percentage or simple measures of Very

Low to Very High, the cells within the grid when combined determine the actual rating of the risk or opportunity

A risk rated as very high and very high have a rating of 0.72 or be in the top quadrant of the "escalation range" agreed with the Project Board

This a technique that is only briefly touched upon in the Prince2 2017 course as Prince2 2017 does not provide specialist techniques

Change Theme – The Change Theme consists of 2 parts:

1. Issue and Change Control
2. Configuration Management

It is also important, actually its fundamental to understand that within Prince2 2017, all changes are classified as Issues as these issues can in fact lead to changes to the project against any of the 6 objectives (Time, Cost, Scope, Quality, Benefits and Risk), so these changes need to managed and controlled. This control is Issue and Change Control within the context of the project

The Configuration Management is effectively version control, every product within a Prince2 2017 project is some form of product, either a Management or a Specialist Product and at some point will be baselined.

Once these products are baselined they are under formal change control, to ensure the integrity of both the product and the project. This formal change control also includes the clearly defined roles and responsibilities relating to who can authorise the change and to what level before the Project Board must become involved. This assumes that some of these responsibilities have in fact been delegated by the Project Board

So it should be clearly understood at the offset, that change and version control go hand in hand and are linked together throughout the lifecycle of the project. We will review each separately

Issue and Change Control – Without effective Change Control the Project Manager will have little control over the users and the scope or direction of the project, which in turn may lead to changes in direction\scope\quality and lead to issues with the objectives Time, Cost and Scope

A user may, in their opinion have a valid change and communicate this directly to the Team Manager and the Team Manager enacts the change, however this is a diversion from the agreed scope and the agreed work package. The aim of the Change Theme is not to stop or prevent changes, but control them and ensure the right changes are approved, part of the role of the Project Manager is to deliver a product that is both fit for purpose (meets the customers' expectations) and supports the realisation of benefits.

The Project Manager and the Project Management Team aim to ensure changes are controlled, identified, assessed, approved and implemented.. They need to be both responsive and also controlled ensuring that changes are approved by the relevant authority before they are produced and paid for

Project Issues – Project Issues can be literally anything and come from any direction (Internal to the project or external from the project) and can be raised by any stakeholder at any time within the Project Lifecycle

Issues are often raised by users, but they can also be raised by members of the specialist teams building\creating the products

Within the Change Theme there are 3 types of issue:

Request for Change – A change to an approved baseline
Off-Specification – Something that has been agreed by the supplier as part of the product (work Package) that has not or will not be delivered (could also be an improvement to the product)
Problem\Concern – Any other issue that requires management actions (formal or informal) to resolve

Request for Change – The Request for Change (RFC) is a change to an agreed baseline, which could be
- An addition to the product
- A removal of something from the baseline
- An amendment to an agreed baseline
- A change in scope or direction
- A suggestion that could lead to any of the above

The obvious source of these are the users, as they often change their minds during the build\development process as they see the product coming to life. This can sometimes be to the benefit of the project, but also can lead to the detriment of the project.

These changes must be fully assessed for their impact upon the objectives and the possible impact upon the Business Justification - the Business Case

Off-Specification – The Off-Specification is where a Team Manager (or Team Member if the Project Manager is the Team Manager) indicates that part of a an agreed Work Package, this is often because of a technical problem or a supplier issue

In most cases this can be resolved quickly by reviewing the scope and the time allocated to the Stage or the Work Package. However if more time and money are required and this is in excess of the agreed tolerances for the Stage, this may not require rework of the actual product but requires more time or money to deliver a product that is aligned to the agreed Work Package.

As the tolerances will be exceed this must be escalated to the next management level – in this instance as it's beyond those agreed limits of the Project Manager, the escalation is to the Project Board or the Change Authority if the Project Board have delegated some of their responsibilities\authority

Problem\Concern – This is effectively any other issue that requires management that is not related to a Request for Change or an Off-Specification.

An example would be, if a key resource within the project who is the only person with a particular skillset, has an accident and can no longer attend work. This is an issue that requires urgent attention and management actions to resolve

Issues Vs Risks – OK, this is something that is often difficult for new Project Managers to understand, there is a clear distinction between Risks and Issues. The simplest way to explain this difference is:

A Risk is something that has not yet happened and an Issue is something that has happened and requires management actions to resolve

An example journey of this in Prince2 is

The organisation plans to send out a marketing campaign to all its existing customers aligned to the financial year end, this is planned for the 1st week of November to highlight major year-end discounts if purchased before Dec 31st.

However, it is understood there may be a strike within the postal workers in November. At this point this is a risk as there is still uncertainty and it is managed as a risk

In October, we find out that the strike is confirmed as negotiations have fallen through, this risk is now an issue and needs formal management to resolve, it is therefore transferred from the Risk Register to the Issue Register

Change Control Procedure – The Prince2 2017 Change Control Procedure has 5 steps (and should be recognisable from the Risk Management Procedure)

These 5 steps are:
1. Capture
2. Assess
3. Propose
4. Decide
5. Implement

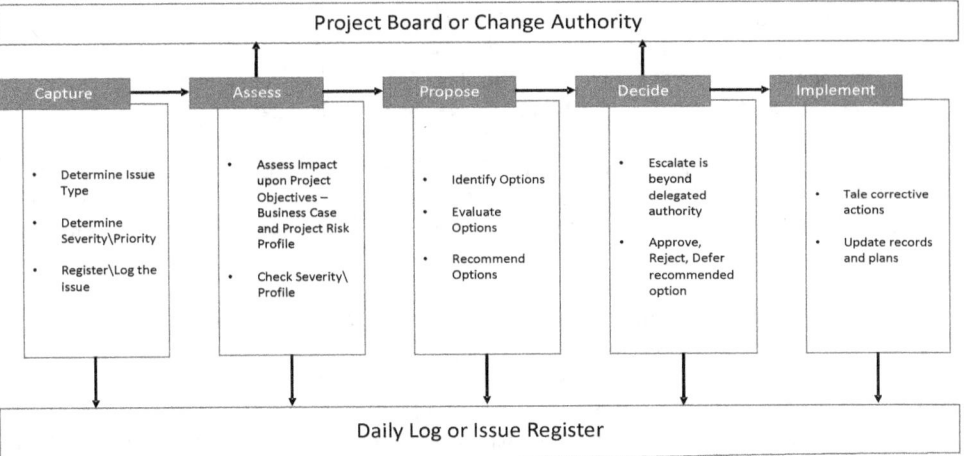

Figure 19 - Prince2 Change Control Procedure

This process works in a similar fashion to the Risk Management Procedure in that,

- **Capture** - When the Issue is captured, the first thing that must be done is to decide whether the issue needs to be formally managed or informally managed. Do we enter it into the Daily Log or the Issue Register, and depending upon the severity or priority of the issue, do we need to create an issue report to enable a more detailed analysis or a pre-emptive report for the Project Board or Change Authority. We must also make an initial assessment of the Priority and Severity of the issue. This is an ideal use of the **MoSCoW** technique (**M**ust have, **S**hould have, **C**ould we have, **W**ould be nice to have or **W**on't have) when assessing the priority, and the use of a simple Critical, Major, Medium or Minor

- **Assess** – When the issue is assessed, this is an evaluation of the impact upon the project objectives (Time, Cost, Scope, Quality, Risks and Benefits), as part of this secondary assessment not that we have more information and a clearer understanding of the issue and its impact, we may revise the priority and severity – this could be raised or lowered depending upon the new information

  We may also request Ad-Hoc advice from the Project Board, especially concerning any issue that could have an impact upon Time, Cost, Scope or Quality

  At this point when we review the Issue, the decision may be taken to transfer it from the Daily Log to the Issue Register again based upon the revised information

- **Propose** – The proposal step includes the identification of the options to resolve the issue, the evaluation of these options and whether they are worth the cost of implementation (in terms of not just cost, but also the resources needed to implement), and recommending an option to enable an informed decision

- **Decide** – The decision what to do with the issue and whether is requires any escalation to the Project Board or the Change Authority, it also depends upon the type of issue and the costs associated as to whether this requires escalation

  Cost and time tolerances are built into the Stages and Work Packages to allow for these types of issues to be managed within the Stage and at the Management Level

  The question the Project Manager asks is "will the resolution of this issue take me beyond the agreed tolerances for the Stage or the Work Package" If it does not then this corrective action can be taken or the decision taken by the Project Manager without the need to escalate

  If escalation is required, then it is escalated to the Project Board or the Change Authority through the use of the issue report

- **Implement** – The implement step is where the agreed actions to resolve the issue are completed, this is known as corrective action. As part of this step the Project Manager will also update all of the relevant documents relating to the issue. This could include:
    - Project Plan
    - Stage Plan
    - Project Product Description
    - Product Description
    - Work Package
    - Stage Plan

This implementation or corrective action must ensure that the baselined products are updated in a controlled manner and all of the appropriate authorisations are completed, if a baselined product is changed, then a new or revised version of the product is created and baselined. The previous version remains unchanged because this is effectively a new or revised product and should be archived for audit purposes

After the issues has closed and the corrective actions undertaken, the issue should be closed and the Project Manager should update the Issue Register to reflect this

Configuration Management (Version Control) – If you have worked on a project before, you will know that in a lot of projects, things change constantly, designs change or the customers' requirements change and the suppliers aren't informed, the end product isn't fit for purpose. This is an clear demonstration of poor change control and poor Configuration Management\Version Control. He end result in this scenario is a failed project

So how should it happen, what should the Project Manager do to ensure the project has effective Configuration Management and Version Control

The first task is to clearly define the Change Control Process and Procedures that the project should adopt. This should be communicated to the entire Project Management Team ensuring that everyone is fully aware of the process to be followed and also the authorisations needed to approve changes

This process will ensure that all changes are controlled and go through a full assessment to understand the impact upon the project objectives, especially those of time and cost.

The version control process will ensure that only the baselined version of the product is the active and approved version, it may put in place controls whereby the historical copies or legacy versions are stored in an archive or in some projects for security, they may even be destroyed to reduce the chances of them being circulated or distributed

On larger projects, it may be necessary to use Configuration Item Records, or more simply explained as Product Records – a record of all products (both Management and Specialist) that will be created as part of this project. This is how the product versions are typically documented, including the change history and links to dependent products or links to products this product is dependent upon

These records are important when there are large numbers of products that could potentially change during the projects lifecycle and are important when individual products are either highly dependent or highly depended upon, this process ensures that any changes to an individual product, can easily be understood which other products and their respective product descriptions should be reviewed as to the impact of the change

This information should also be handed over as part of the project closure, as this formal management is crucial in the BAU process

This is normally part of a database or in its most simplistic form an Excel spreadsheet

Certain Management Products will be subjected to constant change, these are often known as living documents. These products are still under subject to version control and each time a change is made a new version of the product should be compiled or saved and the legacy\historical version archived. This type of version control is lighter than the rigorous version control for the Specialist Products because of the frequency by which they change, examples of these products are:

- The Business Case
- The Project Plan
- Stage Plan
- Project Product Description
- Product Descriptions

Logs and Registers, are not under any type of version control because they will probably change on almost daily basis and this type of version control would become a burden on the Project Manager or Project Support

The Change Control Approach – As mentioned in previous themes (Risk & Quality) this is part of the set of 5 approach documents created as part of the Project Initiation Documentation (PID). The Change Control Approach describes the procedures, techniques, standards and also the levels of authorisation that will be followed to ensure effective change management and version control within the project

Progress Theme – Within the Progress Theme there are:
- Tolerances and exceptions
- Time and event driven controls
- Progress reports

We started this book by reviewing the Business Case and the importance of each of the 6 objectives. Each of these objectives have measures set against them and this in turn means that each of them can have tolerances set against those measurements

The definition of a tolerance in Prince2 2017 is:

"The permissible deviation above and below a plan's target for time and cost without escalating the deviation to the next level of management"

Cost and time tolerances – These can be set for the
- Project – Project level tolerances
- Stage – Stage level tolerances
- Work Packages
- Team Plans

When setting them, they can be expressed in a number of ways:

Absolute tolerances
Cost - +$5,000 \ -$3000
Time - +2 weeks or – 1 week

Relative tolerances
Cost - + or - 5% for time and cost

Quite often the negative tolerances are not used or documented, however some projects, particularly if they are part of a program will need to communicate if they finish early as this may have an impact on other parts of the program

Quality Tolerance - Quality tolerances have a totally different impact and context upon the project and its products. These are documented within either the Project Product Description or the individual Product Descriptions.

An example of this type of tolerance:

The project is developing a new company website, the customer has set a requirement that the landing page must load fully within 5 seconds, however they have set a tolerance of +2 seconds for the page to load giving a maximum time of 7 seconds to load the page. Setting a tolerance like this allows the supplier to develop the website within these tolerances

The tolerances for Time, Cost and Quality tend to be the most used within projects as they can be easily defined and measured.

Other possible tolerances that can be set are:

Benefits Tolerance – The tolerance upon benefits is based upon the fact that benefits are in effect a forecast upon which the Business Case is formed to support the justification of the project. This could be set by Corporate in a standalone project that the benefits are approved on a range of = or – 5% on the forecasted benefits

Any deviation from this would be mean a review of the overall Business Justification

Scope tolerance – Is a little more difficult to assign and would probably be set more in terms of prioritisation of the customers' expectations through the use of the MoSCoW method for the project product and this would be documented within the Project Product Description

Risk Tolerance – This is set by the Project Board during the Initiation Stage and is documented within the Risk Management Approach, the risk tolerance is typically the level of risk that is acceptable to the project board before the risk becomes too risky and not justifiable

This is often expressed as a statement, for example – Any event that makes the system unavailable to the organisation must be escalated

It can also be related to other areas, risks to completion on time, to cost or to the achievement of project quality and within the scope agreed within the constraints of the Business Case

Tolerances can also be traded off against each other or prioritised, for example: If a project has a strict time tolerance – the date of delivery is set and cannot be moved. In this scenario the Project Board may be more flexible in terms of quality or cost to ensure this date is achieved

Setting Tolerances and Delegation - The 4 levels of the Project Management Structure, the tolerances flow down from

- Corporate, Program or Customer – who set Project Tolerances
- Project Board – Set Stage level tolerances
- Project Manager – sets Work Package level tolerances

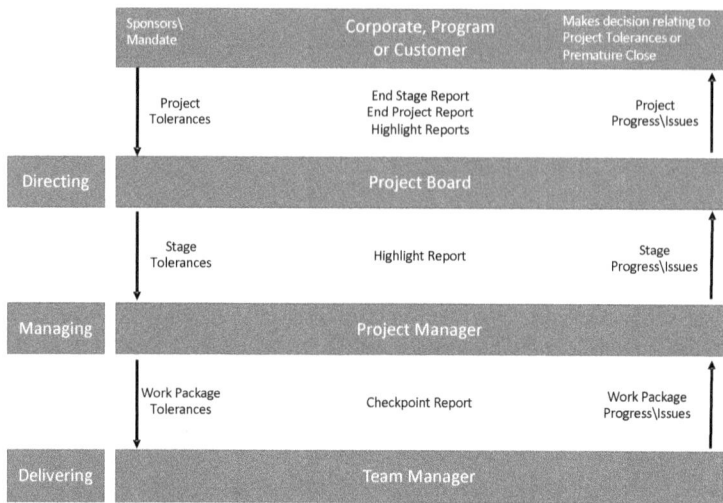

Figure 20 - Project Management Structure

Monitoring Tolerances – as shown in in the figure above, the progress is monitored and reported to the level of management above

The Team Manager reports on Work Package progress and tolerances using the Checkpoint Report, these are then used by the Project Manager to report to the Project Board through the use of the Highlight Report, this also include the information relating to stage progress and tolerances.

The Project Board uses this information to assess the overall project progress and tolerances, then reports to Corporate, Program or Customer. This is normally completed using the End Stage Report but can also be via the Highlight Report if requested

Escalating Issues and Exceptions – it is crucial to the success of the project that there is a clear path to escalate issues and exceptions, this again as with the progress is reported to the next management level

In the event a Team Manager is forecasting to exceed an agreed tolerances (in relation to a Work Package), for example it cannot be completed within the agreed time limits. This must be escalated to the Project Manger via a Project Issue (this is not an exception at this moment in time). If the deviation does not threaten the stage tolerances, the Project Manager can agree and authorise corrective action.

However if it is above the agreed stage tolerances or threatens these tolerances, the Project Manager must escalate this to the Project Board via an Exception Report, if the issue does not threaten the overall project or the tolerances agreed, then the Project Board will ask for an Exception Plan, that when approved will replace the current Stage Plan

In the event that the issue escalated will threaten the overall project tolerances, the Project Board must escalate this to Corporate, Program or Customer again via the Exception Report that has been prepared by the Project Manager. In the event that the issue does not threaten the Business Case (the Project Justification) they normally ask the Project Board to continue with the additional funds\time (or whatever is required to resolve the identified issue) as appropriate, and the Project Board will ask for an Exception Plan to replace the Project Plan.

In the event the escalation threatens the Business Case it is entirely possible that Corporate, Program or Customer will either authorise a major change in scope to bring the project back under control, this is often by descoping major products or deliverables, or will instruct the Project Board to prematurely close the project

It is important to note that all decisions relating to additional budget, major changes ins cope or premature closure are made by Corporate, Program or Customer, as the Project Board acts as the interface between them and the project. These decisions are filtered via the Project Board through the use of the Directing a Project Process

Exceptions are raised as soon as the Project Manager is informed that the tolerance is forecasted to be exceeded, it is essential to remember that this is done as soon as the forecast that the Stage or Work Package within the agreed tolerances, it is important not to wait until the end of the Stage or Work Package and then ask for more time or money, In this instance the Project Manager should be proactive and not reactive

Project Controls – Time and Event Driven Controls – Within a Prince2 2017 project there are 2 types of controls event driven and time driven controls

Event driven controls - Take place when a specific event occurs. This could be, for example, the end stage assessment at the end of a management stage

Time-driven controls - Take place at predefined periodic intervals. This could be, for example, producing monthly highlight reports for the project board or weekly checkpoint reports showing the progress of a work package

Time driven controls are defined within the Communication Management Approach

Whilst the time driven controls are documented within the Communication Management Approach during the Initiation Stage, they are by no means set in stone and cannot be changed. It is prudent to review the requirements for the Highlight Report and its frequency during the project and if required tailor to the coming stage as part of the Managing a Stage Boundary Process

Remember within a Prince2 2017 project, we should only be having progress meetings with the Project Board when Highlight Reports are produced, however if a Work Package was deemed as risky or highly critical. A Checkpoint Report could take the form of a formal meeting, this could be weekly or even daily depending upon the level of risk or criticality within the project

All other controls within Prince2 2017 are classed as event driven control, this means that an event occurs that necessitates the requirement for the report, for example:

- End Stage Report – Managing Stage Boundary Process and the end of the current stage
- End Project Report – the end of the project and the decision to close the project by the Project Board
- Exception Report\Issue Report – an issue has been raised that requires escalation

Progress Reporting – Within Prince2 2017, there are 4 types of progress reports

1. Checkpoint Reports
2. Highlight Reports
3. End Stage Reports
4. End Project Reports

Checkpoint Reports – Are produced by the Team Manager as part of the Managing product Delivery Process. The frequency and contents of the Checkpoint Report are agreed as part of the Team Plan. Typically it will contain a summary of the work completed, the work to be completed in the next reporting period, Work Package progress based upon the actual progress against the plan and any issues or risks under management or that require escalation

Highlight Reports – Are produced by the Project manager during the Controlling a Stage Process, the frequency and contents are agreed and documented as part of the Communication Management Approach during the Initiation Stage and typically contains a summary of this reporting periods progress, a summary of the products or work to be completed in the next reporting period, a summary of risks and issues that require the boards guidance or require their awareness, information upon tolerances in terms of actual and forecasted time and cost information

End Stage Reports – Are produced by the Project Manager during the Managing a Stage Boundary Process, these will typically contain a summary of the stage that is coming to an end based upon the plan that was used as a forecast for its approval. It will also contain an update on Time and Cost and any major issues that were raised or managed during the stage

End Project Report – (Again) is produced by the Project Manager during the Closing a Project Process and typically will contain a summary of the project performance again the objectives (Time, Cost, Quality, Scope, Risk and Benefits), it will also include the formal acceptance reports, lessons report for the overall project, details of any issues and risks and also any follow on actions recommendations that require management post project. It will also contain information on post project risks that will need to be monitored that could have an impact upon the achievement of the benefits

Putting it all together!

IN the next section we will go through a Prince2 2017 project and all of the tasks\activities within each stage. Directing a Project Process does not have a separate section as the activities of this process are covered within the other process chapters

Starting Up a Project Process – As we have already seen, the Starting Up a Project Process or Stage is actually separate from the project and Initiation, it is classified as Pre-Project because it is often a process of estimation or "a finger in air" and the objective is to do the minimum work required to assess if the project is worthwhile and should proceed to the Initiation Stage. It is also an objective of the Starting up a Project Process to stop project and avoid wasting resources on unsound projects.

If the Business Case is not viable, this will become evident quickly and the justification for the overall project should be stopped

For this reason only a draft Project Product Description and Outline Business Case is created as the estimates for time and cost relating to the project are based upon high level estimates and a limited understanding as the customers expiations or requirements at this stage tend to be vague, as do the benefits. The project as a whole is not based upon a detailed project plan and therefore these estimates are often in the range of + or – 50%

The trigger for the Starting Up a Project Process (SU) is the Project Mandate, which as a minimum should identify the Project Executive and provide information upon the project, the terms of reference that give us an overview of the project and its objectives, however – it must be noted that the Project Mandate can come in various forms,

- A verbal instruction
- Email
- Official Project Mandate from a Corporate or Program Board

And contain very little in terms of actual information.

The first activity to be undertaken is

Activity 1 - Appointment of the Project Executive and the Project Manager:
The Project Mandate appoints the Project Executive, who then appoints the Project Manager. The Project Manager then takes the Project Mandate and commences the other activities within the Starting up a Project Process

The Project Manager will open the Daily Log at this point before any other activities are undertaken

Activity 2 - Capture Previous Lessons – The activity of capturing previous lessons commences with the Project Manager reviewing lessons reports from previous similar projects or seeking out Project Managers who have managed similar projects, these lessons may be good or bad but irrespective they may have an impact upon the project and should be captured.

They are entered into the Lessons Log and assessed as to the process, stage or product they may support. This step may take some time and effort from the Project Manager, so it is prudent to review only the most important lessons and possibly focus on meetings with Project Managers at this stage and schedule a more detailed lessons workshop or review once the Authorisation to Initiate has been received from the Project Board

Activity 3 – Design and Appoint the Project Management Team – The Project Management Team Structure, whilst not an official Management Product is part of the Project Initiation Documentation (PID) and should be documented.

At this stage in the project, there may only be the Project Executive and the Project Manager assigned so this documentation will probably only be a skeleton organisation structure with the roles required and will be further updated during the Initiation Stage

Within a larger project, the Project Manager may spend time creating detailed Role and Responsibilities (Job Descriptions) that will be allocated to each person or role contained within the Project Management Team Structure.

In a mature organisation, these may be supplied by the Project Management Office and simply require tailoring to suit the project

Activity 4 - Prepare the Outline Business Case – As we have already reviewed the Outline Business Case and also discussed it in context of the Project Product Description.

The Outline Business Case at this stage is as mentioned based upon vague details and will form the basis of the approval as to whether the project is both viable and worthwhile and is part of the Project Brief.

The Outline Business Case should also contain any information on major risks that could affect its objectives being achieved , whilst we do not have the Risk Register at this moment in time, these risks will be logged within the Daily Log and are transferred to the Risk Register once it is opened within the Initiation Stage

Activity 5 - Select the Project Approach and Assemble the Project Brief – In general the Project Approach reviews the options to deliver the project and how the products will be developed or delivered. For example: will the projects product (the projects output) be an of the shelf product, or will it be developed as a bespoke solution from scratch (something doesn't exist and will be developed or built as a one off system or service), will the resources be in-house, external supplier based resources or a mix of the two.

If we have an external supplier, will they be using a Prince2 2017 based approach, or an Agile based approach for the product development.

It is important to understand this and document this formally and document the Project Approach as the approach may not be obvious to all involved and this will remove any potential for mis-understandings

The Project Brief is a consolidation of documents, it is made up of:

- Project Definition - Explains what the project needs to achieve. It should include:
  - Background
  - Project objectives (covering time, cost, quality, scope, benefits and risk performance)
  - Desired outcomes
  - Project scope and exclusions
  - Constraints and assumptions
  - Project tolerances
  - The user(s) and any other known interested parties
  - Interfaces
- Outline business Case
  - Reasons why the project is needed and the business option selected. This will later be developed into a detailed business case during the initiating a project process
- Project product description
  - Includes the customer's quality expectations, user acceptance criteria, and operations and maintenance acceptance criteria
- Project approach
  - Defines the choice of solution that will be used within the project to deliver the business option selected from the business case. This will take into consideration the operational environment into which the solution must fit and any tailoring requirements (if known)
- Project management team structure
  - A chart showing who will be involved with the project
- Role descriptions
  - These describe the roles of those in the project management team and any other key resources identified at this time
- References
  - These include references to any associated documents or products.

Activity 6 – Plan the Initiation Stage – As part of the authorisation to deliver the project, the Project Board require a plan from the Project Manager for the Initiation Stage, this may not be approved at the same time as the Project Brief as this may be a prerequisite, the approval of the Project Brief is needed to ensure that the Initiation Stage resources can be confirmed. Once this approval is received the Project Manager will start to plan the Initiation Stage

The Project Manager will plan the Initiation Stage and all of the activities that will be undertaken, this will be planned at a level that enables the Project Manager to track the progress on a granular level

The approval of the Project Brief and Initiation Stage Plan also signifies the start of the Directing a Project Process and the official start of the project

It is worth noting, the Authorise Initiation decision that is made by the Project Board is made as a standalone decision and not part of the Managing Stage Boundary

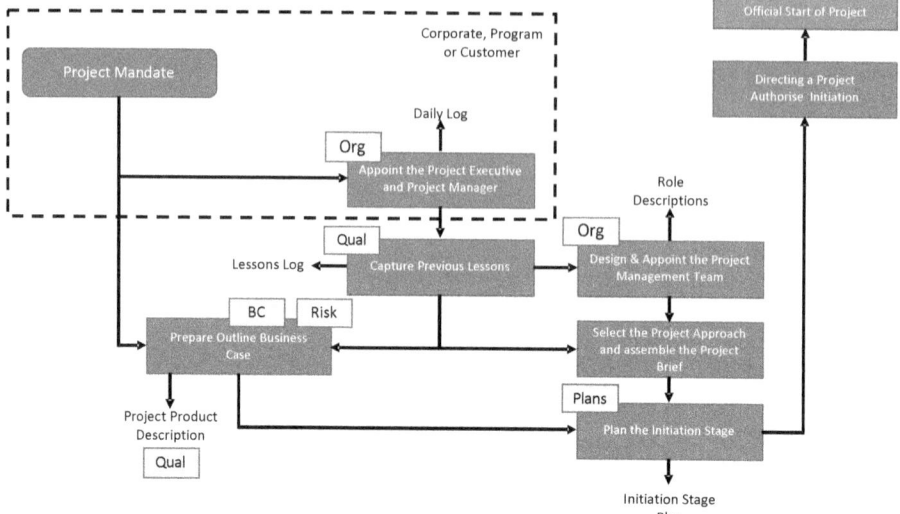

Figure 21 - Starting Up a Project Process

Initiating a Project Process

The project is officially triggered by the Authorisation to Initiate then the Project Board authorises the project at the end of the Starting Up a Project Process

The Project Manager then undertakes the activities of the Initiation Stage

Activity 1 – Agree Tailoring Requirements – The first activity that the Project Manager undertakes is that of agreeing the tailoring requirements. The Project Manager may need to review the project and the current host organisations Project Management Methodology, the project and the approach to determine how the project should be tailored

This will be documented as part of the Project Initiation Documentation – we will review this further later in the book

Activity 2 – Prepare the Management Approaches - The activity if focused upon the creation of the Management Approaches
- Risk Management Approach
- Change Control Approach
- Quality Management Approach
- Communication Management Approach

Which have all been discussed previously, whilst these are being created the registers will be opened or created
- Risk Register – created as part of the Risk Management Approach
- Issues Register - created as part of the Change Control Management Approach

- Quality Register - created as part of the Quality Management Approach

Activity 3 – Setup Project Controls – The Project Controls document the level of control required by the Project Board after the Initiation Stage is completed, it also defines the level of control required by the Project Manager for the work to be undertaken by the Team Manager

This control enables the project to be managed in an effective and efficient manner and supports the Principle of Manage by Exception.

The Project Controls include:
- The frequency and format of communication between the project management levels
- The number of management stages and hence end stage assessments
- Mechanisms to capture and analyse issues and changes
- Mechanisms to monitor tolerances and escalate exceptions
- Tolerances for delegated authority
- How delegated authority from one level of management to another will be monitored

Many of these controls will have been defined in the project's approaches but not necessarily set up. The focus of this activity is to establish such controls and to make sure that they make sense as a coherent set.

These Project Controls will also be defined as part of the Project Initiation Documentation (PID)

Activity 4 – Create the Project Plan – The Project Plan along with the Business Case is one of the main drivers for the project and is created as part of the Initiation Stage, it is not created as part of the Starting up a Project Process as it would simply take too much time and too much effort and given that the level of information within the Start-Up Stage was vague, however we now have a much clearer understanding of both the Project and also the controls needed to deliver it.

The Plan will be created as part of the Product Based Planning Technique with the initial task of creating the Project Product Description as previously discussed as part of the Starting Up a Project Process

The Product Breakdown Structure is a hierarchical representation of the major products and components that will be delivered as part of the project and defines what must be delivered in order to gain acceptance, it is also used to:

- Gain acceptance from the Senior User on the projects scope and requirements
- Define the customers quality expectations
- Define the acceptance criteria, method and responsibilities for the overall project

In some projects the Project Product Description may be created during the Start Up Stage as part of the initiation scoping activities and is refined during the Initiation Stage. It is under formal change control once approved and is reviewed as part of the Managing a Stage Boundary Process and if required updated and approved during the review of the current stage and the approval of the next stage.

It is also used as part of the Closing a Project Process as part of the evaluation of the project and what has been delivered

Once the Project Product Description is created and the major components of the product are understood, the next activity within the Defining and Analysing Products is to create the Product Descriptions, a Product Description is required for product both management and specialist that will be delivered as part of the project.

This will also lead to the creation of the Configuration Item Records, each product that will be created as part of the project requires a Configuration Item Record that will provide a detailed understanding of the product, it's like to other products and the link it as a product and its development status and is linked to Product Status Account (which we will discuss later)

The key input or source of information to these documents is primarily the Project Approach

Activity 5 – Refine the Business Case and Create the Benefits Management Approach – Now that we have created the Project Plan, the Project Product Description, the next activity for the Project Manager is to Refine the Business Case and create the Benefits Management Approach

The Outline Business Case that we created during the Start Up Stage needs to be updated and reflect the estimated time and costs based upon the updated Project Plan, Project Product Description, Approaches and Project Controls

The Detailed Business Case is used by the Project Board during the Directing a Project Process to Authorise the Project and is also used to confirm the continued justification of the project by both the Project Board and the Project Manager

The Detailed Business Case should contain:
- The costs **and** timescale as calculated in the project plan
- The major risks that affect the viability and achievability of the project (from the risk register)
- The benefits to be gained
- The **tolerances** allowed for each of the benefits.

The Project Manager will also create the Benefits Management Approach with the support of the Senior User and any associated Subject Matter Experts
The benefits management approach defines the benefits management actions and benefits reviews that will be putting place to ensure that the project's outcomes are achieved and confirm that the project's benefits are realised

A benefits management approach includes the following:
- The scope of the benefits management approach covering what benefits are to be managed and measured post project
- Who is accountable for the expected benefits – normally the Senior User but this may be delegated
- How to measure achievement of expected benefits, and when they can be measured
- What resources are needed – IT\HR for report or extract etc

- Baseline measures from which the improvements will be calculated
- How the performance of the project's product will be reviewed.

Activity 6 – Assemble the Project Brief – The purpose of the Project Initiation Documentation also known as the PID is to define the project and forms the basis for its management and an assessment of its overall success

The primary uses for the PID within a Prince2 2017 project are:
- ensure that the project has a sound basis before asking the project board to make any major commitment to the project
- act as a base document against which the project board and project manager can assess progress, issues and ongoing viability questions
- provide a single source of reference about the project so that people joining the 'temporary origanisation" can quickly and easily find out what the project is and how is being managed

The PID is a "living" document and should always reflect or contain the most up to date information in relation to the plans, controls, finances and will be updated during the project primarily during the Managing a Stage Boundary Process

At the completion of the Initiation Stage the PID is baselined and preserved as the baseline to measure the project during the Closing a Project Process

The PID contains the following documents or information:
- Project Definition
- Project Approach
- Business Case
- Role Descriptions
- Quality Management Approach
- Change Management Approach
- Risk management Approach
- Communication Management Approach
- Project Plan
- Tailoring

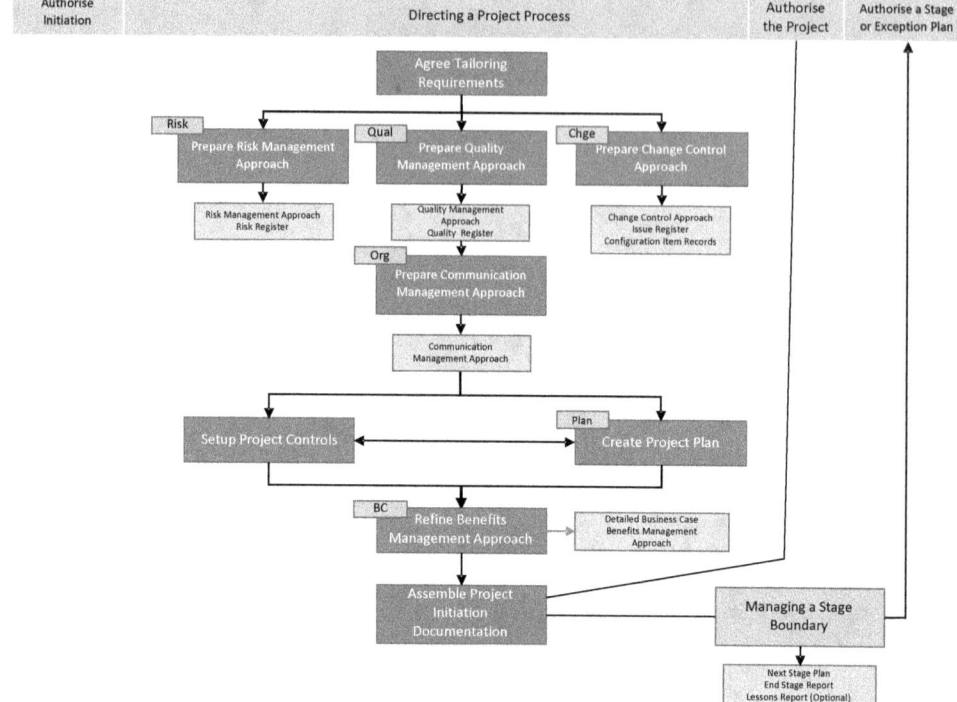

Figure 22 - Initiating a Project Process

Managing a Stage Boundary Process – This is a smaller version of the Managing a Stage Boundary Process as this is the completion of the first stage of the project and links directly to the Directing a Project Process whereby the output is the Authorisation to Deliver the Project from the Project Board

The Project Manager will create the Next Stage Plan and in cases this will include the End Stage Report, as the registers have only just been created or opened, in essence the Project Manager will not need to undertake any major reviews of these however it is prudent to review the Risk Register for any risks that could affect the next stage of the project

It is also feasible that the project could lose the justification or viability, this could be for any number of reasons, for example: lack of clarity has led to increased costs, supplier issues, a change in organisation direction effecting the business case, hence one of the questions the Project Board will ask during a Managing Stage Boundary is about the continuation of the Project, in the event it is not then the decision to prematurely close the project is an option open to the Project Board although it is rare for this to happen, however at this stage of the project this would be very rare

If the Project Board agree that the project is sound and Authorises the Project, this decision effectively authorising the delivery or creation of the Specialist Products

The next process that is triggered upon receiving authorisation is the Controlling a Stage Process

Controlling a Stage Process – The Controlling a Stage Process (CS) is essential to the overall success of the project, this is the reporting of progress, the control of the project and the associated issues, risks, tolerances but more importantly the link between the Project Manager and the Team Manager through the Work Packages

The Project Manager will focus upon the Specialist Products through the creation of the Work Packages, which is effectively a negotiation of the Work Package based upon the contents of the Product Description that has been agreed by the Senior User (or their approved representative)

This agreement leads straight into the Managing Product Delivery Process (MP), so this makes sense to review this process and then review the remainder of the Controlling a Stage Process (CS)

Figure 23 - Managing product Delivery Process

Managing Product Delivery Process – The Managing Product Delivery Process commences when the Project Manager Authorises a Work Package as part of the Controlling a Stage Process

There are 3 activities within the Managing Product Delivery Process (MP), these are:
- Accept a Work Package
- Execute a Work Package
- Deliver Work Package

The main purpose of the Managing Product Delivery Process is to ensure that only work that it authorised is being worked upon and the role of the Team Manager is coordinate this work and report upon its progress to the Project Manager

Activity 1 – Accept a Work Package – The process of Accepting the Work Package should be through that of negotiation whereby the Project Manager creates the contents of the Work Package based upon the Product description with a clear focus upon
- Quality Criteria (prioritised)
- Quality Methods
- Quality Tolerances
- Quality Responsibilities

However there may also be supporting information from secondary sources, designs, architects drawings, legislations etc. These along with the associated Product Description should be included with the Work Package

The reason for the negotiation, is that this process works better in an environment where people work together rather that of a being told or mandated to complete the Work Package

The Team Manager will review the contents of the Work Package and clarify with the Project Manager what is to be achieved in relation to Time, Cost and Scope and also discusses\review any constraints and agree any tolerances

At this point the Team Manager will review the Quality Responsibilities (those authorised to accept the Work Package on behalf of the Senior User) and if required review them with Project Assurance

The Project Manager will then create the Team Plan showing the details in relation to the Products associated with the Work package,
- What will be created
- Details of any reporting requirements and the contents of the Checkpoint Report

The Team Manager will then:
- Review any risks associated with the team Plan and raise them to the Project Manager
- Update the Quality Register and Configuration Item Records

The final step is to agree the Work Package and commence execution

Activity 2 – Execute Work Package – This is where the Specialist Products relating to the project are finally created, procured or modified and this work is undertaken by the Team Members .

Whilst this work in undertaken, the Team Manager will report upon the progress using the Checkpoint Report at the agreed frequency contained within the Team Plan, note that the Checkpoint report will vary depending upon the project and the team completing the work. In some circumstances this will be a formal report from an external suppliers, in others it could simply be an email confirming the progress from an internal supplier (IT or HR for example)

It is also key to note that during this process it is the Team Manager who is responsible for the Quality Control as defined within the Quality Theme and in Figure 12 earlier in the book. Prince2 suggests that there is no reason for the Project Manager to be stuck in the middle of the execution process and continually reviewing or checking upon the development status and associated quality. It recommends that it is much more streamlined and effective if the Team Manager liaises directly with the Quality Reviewers, however this must have effective Change Control and Change Authority levels defined and documented to retain control over Time, Cost and Scope.

The final activity within the Execute Work Package is to complete the Quality Review of the associated product, this is undertake using the Quality Review Technique. Within Prince2 2017 there are 2 types of quality methods
- In Process – Quality reviews during the development\creation of the Specialist Products are agreed points or intervals
- Appraisal – The Quality review is undertaken to assess the final or finished product for completeness and reviewing if it is fit for purpose

The actual Quality Review is undertaken using the Prince2 2017 Quality Review Technique, which in the absence of any other process or procedures complements the Products Descriptions and Work Package activities

The Quality Review aims to assess the products conformity against the agreed criteria as documented in the Product Description, ensure that those Quality Reviewers are included within the process and provide confirmation that the product is accepted and fit for purpose

The 4 roles required for an effective review are:
1. Chair – responsible for the overall conduct of the meeting, ensures the review is undertaken properly.
2. Reviewer – Represents the Senior User and reviews the products against the Acceptance Criteria agreed
3. Admin – Provides administrative support for the meeting to the Chair and records the results or actions from the meeting
4. Presenter – Represents the Senior Supplier and those who have created the product

As with all roles within Prince2 2018, the above are roles and not people. These can be combined as

1. Chair\Reviewer
2. Presenter\Admin

Once the Work Package is reviewed and accepted, this leads to the final activity of the Managing product Delivery Process, which is to hand over the Deliver Completed Work Package to the Project Manager

Activity 3 – Deliver Completed Work Package – This is effectively handing over the Acceptance Records to the Project Manager, most projects will no longer have actual products to hand over due to their very nature. The benefit of using the Quality Review Technique during the Work Package execution is that product that is handed to the Project Manager is completed and accepted having been fully reviewed by those representatives of the Senior User

This leads us directly back into the Controlling a Stage Process to continue with the remainder of the activities that will be undertaken by the Project Manager

Controlling a Stage Process Continued - The Work Package process is effectively made up of three activities from the perspective of the Project Manager, these are

Activity 1 – Authorise Work Package – As we have just seen the Work Package process above was all from the perspective of the Team Manager and is started by the process of Accepting a Work Package. The Work Package process will vary from each project and in essence as every project is unique, there could be one Work Package or multiple Work Packages.

There can be multiple Work Packages running concurrently and they can span multiple management stages, unlike Management Stages where can only be one running

The Project manager needs to manage these effectively and control them with the Team Manager

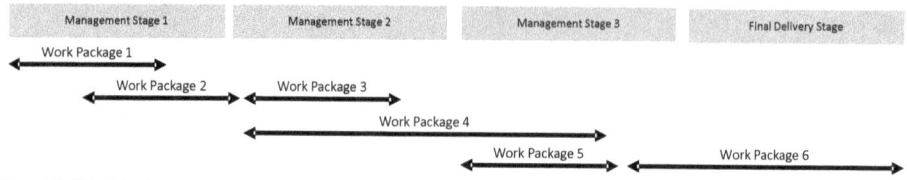

Figure 24 - Work Packages

It is crucial to the project's success that the Project Manager works with the Team Managers when creating the Stage Plan, 2 many products being created will introduce additional potential risks or even issues!

Activity 2 – Review Work Package – This again is the mirror perspective of the Team Managers Executing Work Package. The Team Manager reports progress to the Project Manager using the Checkpoint Reports, this enables the Project Manager to review progress, asses risks or issues relating to the associated Work Package and report progress to the Project Board using the data received to the Project Board using the Highlight Reports

The Project Manager will also update the Stage Plan, Quality Register, Risks Register (As necessary), Configuration Item Records with the information contained within the Checkpoint Report

Activity 3 – Receive Completed Work Package – You should see a pattern forming now, this again is the mirror of the Deliver Completed Work Package, the Work Package is effectively completed totally now and has been executed, reviewed and accepted. The products have been approved by the representatives of the Senior User.

The Project Manager will receive the Acceptance Records for those products, it is crucial these are reviewed and stored, as these are key for the Closing a Project Process and acceptance of the final project product from the Senior User

The final activities are
- Capture and Examine Issues and Risks
  - Escalate Issues and Risks
- Review Stage Status
- Report Highlights
- Take Corrective Action

We will review each of these activities next

Activity 1 – Capture and Examine Issues and Risks – Whilst the Project Manager will focus heavily on the Work Packages, it is crucial they not forger the other activities. The Project Manager also needs to manage the issues and risks on an ongoing basis, this effectively involves monitoring those issues and risks that are already under formal management within the Issue Register and Risk Register but also the identification and assessment of new issues and risks.

Dependent upon the severity of the issue or risk, an Issue Report of Exception Report may be required

The Issues and Risks are managed using the processes documented within both the Risk Management Approach and the Change Control Approach

Activity 2 – Review Stage Status – Reviewing Stage Status is a much broader and in depth review of the stage that is in progress and not only covers the Work Packages, but also covers everything relating to that stage (Issues, Risks Etc) This is possibly the most important activity the Project Manager undertakes and is essentially ensuring that the stage and the deliverables (Work Packages) remain on track or aligned to the objectives (Time, Cost, Scope, Quality, Benefits and Risks)

In a perfect world the Project Manager will take a step back and assign time each week to review the stage and the project, this allows the Project Manager to avoid being "stuck in the detail" if you have ever heard the saying "can't see the wood for the tree's" this is essentially why the Project Manager needs to set time aside to review the stage, without this separation the Project Manager will start to miss obvious things, like risks or issues and these could potentially jeopardise the overall project

This process of reviewing the stage, issues, risks and Work Packages is fundamental to the role of the Project Manager and actually managing the project itself. As a professional Project Manager, I put a meeting with myself for 1 hour every morning and blocked this time to allow me to review the status of the project. This is something you will learn with time and maturity and find your own process of this reviewing the stage

As part of this process, the Project Manager may also liaise with the Project Board and ask for Ad-Hoc advice or guidance in relation to issues or risks

Activity 3 – Reporting Highlights – The timings for this will be unique to the project and also be dependent upon the confidence of the Project Board in the Project Team. In some circumstances the Project Board may ask for more frequent reports again, based upon the Project and the Team. This as we have discussed is documented within the Communications Management Approach, in most projects this report is completed fortnightly

The Highlight Report allows the Project Manager to report progress without the need to have formal meetings with the Project Board.

Typically the Highlight Report will contain information on the following:
- Current Reporting Period
- Next Reporting Period
- Risks
- Issues
- Additional Information
- Optional –
  - Financial Information

Activity 4 – Taking Corrective Action – Whilst reviewing the Stage Status, the Project manager will be constantly looking at the project and asking one very simple question

"are we where we should be and will we finish this stage within the agreed time and cost tolerances"

If the answer is a simple yes, then all is good and no corrective action is needed, however if the answer is no for whatever reason, for example: A Work Package is forecasted that it cannot be completed within the agreed tolerances. The Project Manager will review this and if they are happy this will not affect the overall stage tolerances, the Project Manager can take corrective action (within the agreed tolerances for the stage) with agreement from the Team Manager which will result in possibly reworking the affected Work Package(s)

If the Project Manager assessing the Issue or Risk, and it cannot be resolved within the agreed tolerances, this must be escalated to the Project Board using the Exception Report. This could be for any number of reasons,

- It could be simply insufficient time or money to complete the stage of the Work Packages,
- The Checkpoint Reports are indicating that the deliverables are slipping and there is now a concern that the deliverable will not be completed on time
- An Issue or Risk relating to the stage requires direction and escalation

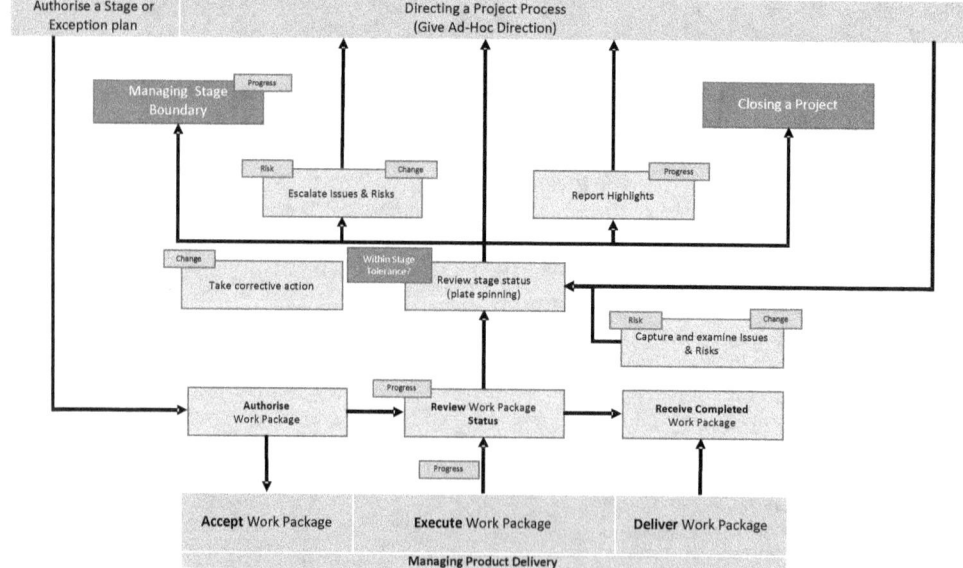

Figure 25 - Controlling a Stage Process

Managing a Stage Boundary Process – As previously discussed earlier in this section of the book, at or near the end of the current stage the Project Manager will commence the Managing a Stage Boundary Process, unlike the Managing a Stage Boundary Process at the end of the Initiation Stage, this is now the full process that it undertaken, however if this is the final delivery stage the Managing a Stage Boundary Process is replaced by the Closing a Project Process

The activities within the Managing a Stage Boundary Process are:

- Plan the Next Stage
- Update the Project Plan
- Update the Benefits Management Approach
- Review (and update) the PID
- Report Stage End
- End Stage Assessment
- Produce Exception Plan (if required)

Activity 1 – Plan the Next Stage – The first task for the Project Manager is to create the Next Stage Plan, this is often undertaking using the Product Based Planning Process to allow the Project Manager to understand both the products needed, their sequence and any dependencies between them.   As part of the Product Based Planning process, new products that are identified will need to have Product Description created (or updated) along with Configuration Item Records

The Product Description will need to have the relevant quality criteria defined and entered into the Quality Register.

The roles assigned and required will also be reviewed, new members will be introduced into the Project Management Team. Especially in the role of Senior User, Senior Supplier or Team Manager. This is primarily because the project is moving from one delivery stage to another

Activity 2 – Update the Project Plan – Once the Project Manager has created the Stage Plan, the Project Plan will be updated to reflect the actual progress to date with a focus upon Time and Cost and update it with a revised cost estimates for the remainder of the project. This is based upon the revised information from the planning undertaken during the planning for the next stage

Activity 3 – Update the Benefits Management Approach – This may not be required in the early stages of the project, and in some projects will not be required until the final stages. Pricne2 2017 alludes that benefits are realised post project, but this is not the case in all projects and benefits can be incrementally achieved.

For example, Business Process Improvement projects, can deliver benefits in small increments that when combined deliver the full forecasted benefits that were used as part of the projects justification

In the scenario where benefits are incremental the Project Manager will update the Benefits Management Approach to reflect the benefits that have been delivered for measurement, this will include the measurement process, tools, responsibilities, timings etc

This may in turn also mean the Business Case needs to be updated to reflect this information, this is part of the Project Initiation Documentation (PID)

Activity 5 – Review (and update) the PID – The Project Manager will review the entire contents of the PID to ensure they still accurately reflect the project and its management team. This review is undertaken to ensure the assigned roles remain accurate and any changes are approved.

The 4 approach documents will also be reviewed to ensure the Project Controls remain effective

Activity 6 – Report Stage End – One of the main purposes\reasons for the Managing a Stage Boundary Process is to report the end of the current management stage, this is done in the form of the End Stage Report. The End Stage Report provides the Project Board with a summary of the projects progress and will document any updates to the Business Case, Benefits Management Approach, PID or the Project Plan

At this point, the Project Manager will also undertake "housekeeping or maintenance" on the Registers and the Logs, the Project Manager will update the Lessons Log with any information or lessons. These lessons are primarily documented for the benefit of the project and its future stages and any lessons that will benefit the host organisation or projects

An optional report as part of the End Stage Report is the Lessons Report, which documents lessons that will benefit the project or the organisations process

Activity 7 – End Stage Assessment – The End Stage Assessment is undertaken by the Project Board based upon the End Stage Report and the Next Stage Plan created by the Project Manager.

The Project Board are primarily focused upon the Continued Business Justification and are asking the questions

- Does the project remain justified
- Do we accept the risks associated with the project and continuing
- Can the products be delivered to time cost and quality

If the Project Board agrees that this is the case, they will authorise the Next Stage Plan and authorise the closure of the current stage

In the event that the project is not going well, the Project Board will review the project and its scope, with a view to potentially reducing the scope to allow the project to complete on time and to budget and therefore maintain the business justification – this scope review normally leads a reduction in scope and the project being replanned.

However if the project is encountering serious problems, the decision by the project could be to Prematurely Close the Project. This would decision would require support from Corp, Prog or Customer and the decision filtered down to the Project Manager and members of the Project Management Team

Leading to the final activity in Controlling a Stage, where the project is forecasted not be completed within the tolerances agreed

Activity 8 – Produce an Exception Plan – It must be remembered, the Exception Plan is inly produced at the request of the Project Board, and in some circumstances they may not actually ask for one but simply approve the increase in a tolerance to allow the stage to be completed

The first step in the exception process is to create an Exception Report

Activity 9 – Produce an Exception Plan – If the project is not going well, and the Project Manager is forecasting that the stage or even worse the project itself, this should be escalated to the Project Board as soon as possible to allow them to make an informed decision how to proceed.

The Project Board are informed through the Exception Report, in the scenario where the projects justification is not threatened and therefore it is no longer justifiable and can be recovered with additional time or money therefore increase the tolerances for time or cost and this can be allocated by the Project Board (and the tolerance is not a project level tolerance), they will ask the Project Manager to create an Exception Plan.

This is created as part of the Managing a Stage Boundary Process as the process to create the Exception Plan is the same set of activities the Project Manager will undertakes when transitioning from one delivery stage to the next

The Exception Plan is an unplanned event, and Exception Plan is created to allow the stage that is in review to be completed, through the additional of time, money or even a reduction in scope

The Exception Plan is reviewed by the Project Board and if approved replaces the current stage plan to allow the stage to be completed, additional activities or deliverables may be required to complete the stage and the Project Manager will review the contents of the PID, the Benefits Management Approach etc

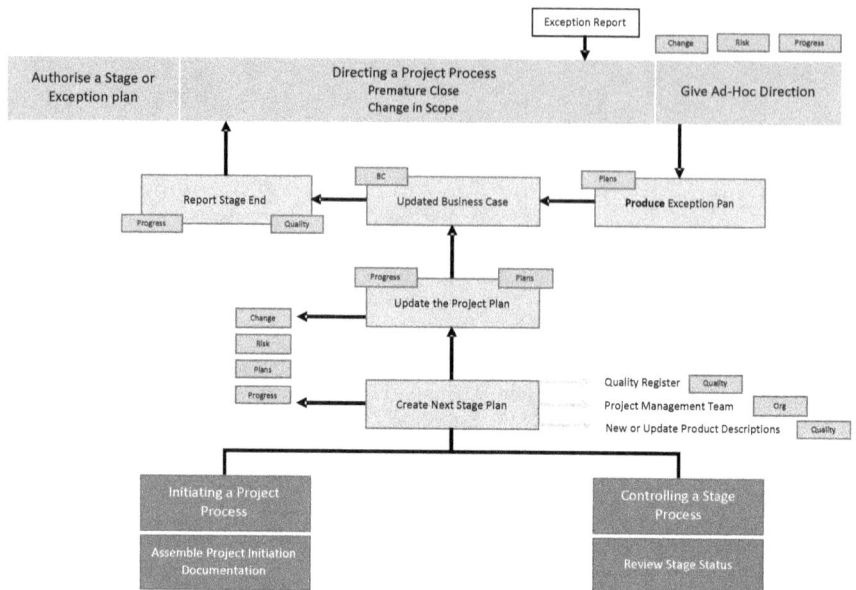

Figure 26 - Managing a Stage Boundary Process

Closing a Project Process – as mentioned already, in the final delivery stage of the project, the Managing a Stage Boundary Process is replaced by the Closing a Project Process and the Project Board is primarily interested in 2 things

- Has the project been a success
    - Has it been delivered to Time, Cost, Scope, Quality, Risk and will Benefits be achieved
    - Is the projects output (the Specialist Product) a success
        - The evaluation of this is based upon user acceptance, operational acceptance and will deliver the expected benefits

Both of these questions can only be answered at the closure of the project and the benefits realisation question will remain open (potentially) long after the actual project has been closed

In truth most projects struggle at this point, for a number of reasons,
- Difficulty in transitioning the Specialist Products to operation support
- Unclear end to the project in development\software based projects
- Scope was not clear enough and the end product is not accepted

In truth, Prince2 2017, there is no magic bullet or guidance on how to remedy these issues, what it does say and recommend is that the Project should have a clearly defined end point that is planned and aligned to the estimates for time and cost

It should always be totally clear to the Project Board, that when the project is closed the Project Management Team is disbanded and there will be no further resources available, the only resources remaining will be Corp, Prog or Customer who are primarily focused upon the benefits and the reviews to measure the return of investment that was the basis of the projects original justification, this reporting is normally undertaken by the Senior User and Prince2 2017 states that the Senior User is "Held accountable for the benefits"

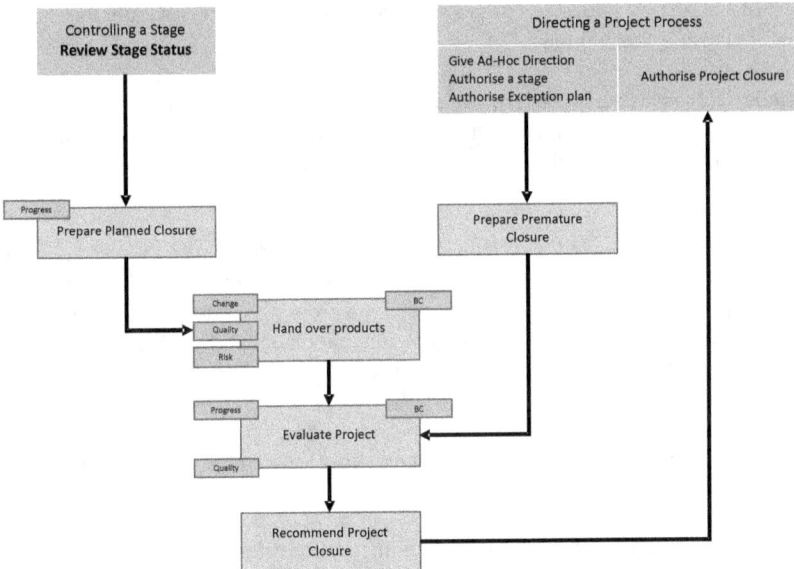

Figure 27 - Closing a Project Process

Prepare Planned Closure – In the scenario where the project has ran its course as planned or with minor modifications to time, cost or scope. The Project Manager will commence the planned closure process and update the Project Plan, Benefits Management Approach and Business Case with the actuals for the time and cost relating to the overall project

Prepare Premature Closure – From the Authorisation to Initiate the Project it can be closed prematurely at any point and this is triggered by the Project Board in response to the project no longer having a valid justification, this notification from the Project Board can

- Be in the for of Ad-Hoc guidance relating to an external event
- Response to an Exception Report
- Reviewing the Projects Business Case again risks or issues
- Reviewing the Projects Business Case during the stage boundary process

The Premature Closure Process is actually not a cut down or reduced version of the Closing a Project Process and dependent upon where the project is in its lifecycle, it can actually mean more work to close the project.

The Project Manager will assess the Specialist Products that

- Have been completed and accepted
- Are in development, procurement or being built
- Have not started

This is undertaken to assess if any of the Specialist Products can provide any of the identified benefits on their own and if so additional work instructions are created to allow them to be handed over into but operational use within the user community and operational support

The Project Manager may also need to assess and review any contracts to understand the impact of the premature closure of the project

The remainder of the closure process remains the same for both premature closure and planned closure, and Prince2 2017 recommends this is undertaken in a controlled manner and that all documents are updated and archived in the event the project is restarted or opened again in the future

Hand Over Products – The main focus upon the Hand Over Products process is to ensure that the Specialist Products are handed over to both the operational (user community) and the maintenance (support teams) before the closure of the project and the Project Management Team disbands, this may be a complete handover upon completion or a phased handover of products as they are completed. In either case this would be documented within the Project Approach and the Project Plan

In the case of the Premature Closure (as mentioned above) some products may need to handed over as part of the closure process

The Project Manager will obtain the formal acceptance records for the Specialist Products that were completed as part of the Managing product Delivery process, these are from both the user and support community

Any issues that are open or remain open in relation to the Specialist Products, for example any products that were accepted with conditions (items yet to be delivered etc) will be assessed and transferred to the Follow-on Action Recommendations to be passed onto the relevant team(s) to monitor post project. This allows the Issue Register to be closed

It is also crucial that the Project Manager reviews the Benefits Management Approach and updates it to include the post project activities to measure the benefits, and this will be passed onto Corp, Prog or Customer by the Project Board who will monitor the benefits

Evaluate the Project – IN truth evaluating the project is quite simple, the Project Board will simply review how successful the project is based upon the original estimates for Time, Cost and Quality given the Benefits will be measured post project and reported upon by the Senior User

The Project Manager will use various management products when evaluating the project and some of these actions\methods are:
- Review the original contents of the PID (baselined upon completion of the Initiation Stage)
- Review any approved changes (against the baselined PID and the current or final version of the PID)
- Review the Acceptance Records and identify any outstanding actions or comments
- Review the Lessons Log

The Project Manager will use this information to prepare the End Project Report, this will contain any Follow-On Action Recommendations and the Lessons Report for the overall project (which at this point is not optional)

The End Project Report should be an honest report containing information on both what went well, what went badly and what can be learned from the project to aid future projects and improve the host organisations project delivery processes

Recommend Project Closure – Once the Specialist Products have been handed over and the Project Manager has completed the evaluation of the project, the Project Manager will formally recommend to the Project Board and primarily the Project Executive to close the project

If the Project Board agree, they will inform Corp, Prog or Customer that the Project is now closed and notify the Project Manager to disband the Project Management Team

At this point, the final task for the Project Manager is to close all of the projects registers and logs and archive the project documentation

Tailoring Prince2 2017

Anyone who knows Prince2 already will know the most common statement (which was simply inaccurate) was that it was unwieldy and bureaucratic, however this is simply not the case and this is also one of the biggest changes from Prince2 2009 to Prince2 2017, it now includes minimum requirements for the Themes and the Purpose and Objectives for the Processes. Which together show the bare minimum requirements that a project needs to meet to be able to demonstrate that it is being managed as a Prince2 2017 project

In essence, if you do not tailor Prince2 2017, your using a sledgehammer to crack a walnut

The only non-negotiable of the integrated elements are the 7 Principles, that MUST be applied

The next section is aimed at showing how a project can be tailored, in essence this is often based upon common sense and as a rule, if it does not make sense to you as the Project Manager, or there is no logic why something is being done – then why are you doing it?

If this is happening, the answer is normally either:
- There is limited understanding of Prince2 2017
- There is limited understanding of what can be tailored within Prince2 2017 or how it can be tailored
- The organisation does not understand Prince2 2017

And this lack of understanding leads to confusion and doing things that are unnecessary, which in turn could lead to additional costs or time

So what are the basics of tailoring within Prince2 2017

Naming Conventions (Roles & Products)

Naming Conventions (Roles & Products) – In the classroom and the exam, Prince2 2017 expects roles and documents to be names and aligned to the official manual, however in the real world it simply doesn't care. The key criteria is that a standard methodology and terminology is being followed and if possible, there is a glossary to show the Prince2 2017 name and the organisations naming convention

For example –

Prince2 2017 Name	Organisation Name
Outline Business Case	BC1
Detailed Business Case	BC2

The documents provide the same function within the project methodology, but are named based upon the organisation needs

This can however cause confusion when working with external suppliers or temporary resources, which again is another reason to have the glossary of terms

Management Products

Management Products -The official Prince2 2017 manual contains an appendix that has an example of each of the management products and the composition of each of these products.

However! These are examples and the question of how formally or blindly you need to follow these examples and document for every project and in cases the simple truth is less is more!

It may be prudent to decide that on a simple, small project that these document are combined to simplify the management and reduce the burden on the Project Manager, versus a large complex project where it is more prudent to include all of the management products to ensure the projects is focused upon meeting the objectives of Time, Cost, Quality, Scope, Benefits and Risks

In simple truth, again Prince2 2017 means you do not need to have the documents named to match the Prince2 2017 naming conventions and you also do not need to include the headings all of the time on all projects, Tailoring should be appropriate to the project and its complexity, risks, and the benefits being delivered

As always, a key skill is common sense is the driver in relation to tailoring of the Management Products and it should also be remembered that Management Products can be combined or even split into separate documents. IN my own projects I combine the Risk Register, Actions\Assumptions Register, Issues Register and Dependencies Register into a single document called the RAID Log to simplify the management or Risks and Issues

Management Products are often referred to as documents, however they can be presented and approved in any format, a Business Case for example could be a Word Document, PowerPoint Presentation or even an Excel Spreadsheet. The key to tailoring is documenting this within the Project Controls and the associated Quality Management System

Processes and Activities – Any activity or process within Prince2 2017 can be combined or split into more detailed processes or activities, the question when doing this is to question if the process or activity makes sense to the project and its context. Larger projects can have processes or activities separate or combined and adversely on smaller projects, you can combine processes or activities

Again, it is crucial to document this tailoring within the Project Control and baseline them as part of the Initiation Process

Simple Projects – So with all of the tailoring open to you as the Project Manager, the starting point will always be the project itself, its size, its complexity, the benefits associated.

A simple project is easily defined as:
- Short in duration – 6-12 weeks for example
- Low complexity – one or 2 specialist products for example
- Low cost
- Low risk

The definition of all of the above will be unique to the individual organisation and as such there is no "one size fits all" to define a simple project, and the above markers or measure are the criteria within Prince2 2017

Prince2 2017 has 4 main areas for tailoring within a simple project:

Organisation – within a Prince2 2017 project it is actually possible to have a minimum of 3 people to deliver the project successfully. This is based upon the Supplier being an external organisation or provider, therefore the Senior Supplier is the 3rd person.

The Executive and the Senior User roles can be combined and represented by a single individual

This forms the Project Board, the members of the Project Board undertake their own Project Assurance activities and Change Authority

The Project Manager, would then provide the management of the actual project and undertake the role of the Team Manager working directly or liaising with the Team Members. The Project Manager will also undertake the role of Project Support

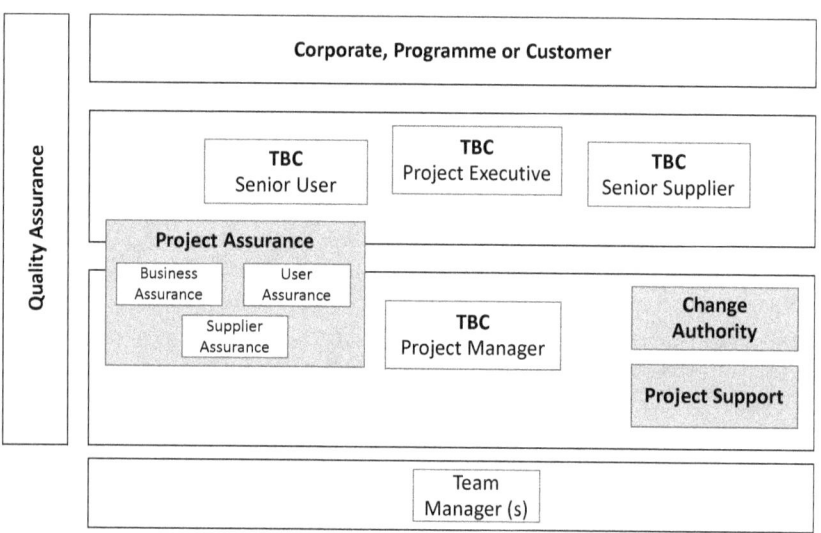

Figure 28 - Project Management Team Structure

The Project Management Team can effectively be 3 people to manage the delivery of the overall project

Stages – The Minimum stages within a Prince2, which effectively means that the Starting Up a Project Process and Initiating a Project Process within a simple project can be combined with the output being the Authorisation to Deliver the Project from the Project Board. This constitutes a single stage

The 2nd stage would be the delivery stage where the Specialist Products are created, purchased or built and upon completion the Closing a Project Process would be commenced to complete the handover of the products and the evaluation of the project

This breaks the project into 2 simple stages that will then greatly reduce the number of Management Products and therefore the management burden on the Project Manager

Management Products – Given the project is now being managed with a simplified Project Management Team and using only 2 stages, the next area is the Management Products.

Given the simple nature of the Project the following 4 products should be sufficient to manage project effectively

Project Initiation Documentation (PID) – The PID as a minimum should contain
- Some sort of documented and approved Business Case, which as a minimum should contain at least the justification, benefits and costs associated with the project
- A document Project Plan – even if this is at a high level given the simplicity of the project
- A Project Product Description to allow clarity on what is being delivered and what success looks like
    - This could also contain individual Product Descriptions as needed

In this format, it would not be unusual for the PID to be a single document presented to the Project Board to enable them to provide Authorisation to Deliver the Project

Highlight Reports – Allow the Executive and Project Board to monitor the progress of the project during the delivery stage, these will be linked to the Checkpoint Reports received from the Team Members which in a simple project may be communicated at a weekly meeting between the Project Manager and the Team Members

Daily Log – This as we are aware, is the Project Managers diary and irrespective of the scale of the project, the Project Manager will always have a Daily Log to informally manage issues, risks or changes, lessons etc and it can also act a s a diary for reminders

End Project Report – As part of ensuring the project is closed off correctly and the products are handed over, the End Project Report should contain
- Written acceptance of the Specialist Products
- Evaluation of the Project overall

So in essence, the project is
1. Ran using 4 people within the Project Management Team
2. Has 2 Stages
3. Has 4 Management Products

This is fundamentally a very small project, in truth you should still have the 4 Project Approaches agreed and some form of Risk and Issue Management Process agreed, this again improves the overall chances of successfully delivering the project

Is your Project a Prince2 2017 Project

The next chapter is a very simple clean set of 7 questions that a Project Manager should be able to ask to affirm if the Project is being delivered as a Prince2 2017 Project. These questions answer whether the 7 Principles are being applied and therefore if the project is being ran as a best practice project

Ser	Question	Yes\No	Remarks
	Continued Business Justification principle		
1	Has the Business Case been properly prepared and approved		
2	Is it being reviewed and updated		
3	Are the Benefits documented and forecasted		
4	Can they be used to assess the projects Continued Justification and if necessary allow the decision to close the project		
5	Are Benefit Reviews being held and benefits reported		
6	Has the Business Case been properly prepared and approved		
	Manage by Stages		
1	Is the Project being split into stages (minimum of 2)		
2	Are separate (detailed) Stage plans being documented and used		
3	Are there clearly management boundaries allowing control points or decision points		
4	Are ongoing viability assessment being held at the boundaries reviews based upon the Business Case		
	Manage by Exception		
1	Are time tolerances for Time and Cost being set at project\stage and work package levels		
2	Is RAG reporting being used - If so. are the RAG definitions documented		
3	Are regular meetings held with the Project Board - are these meeting productive, decisions being made and not simply progress meetings		
	Defined Roles and Responsibilities		
1	Are the roles clearly defined and differentiated - Corp, Prog or Customer - Project Board - Project Manager		
2	Is independent Project Assurance in place		
3	Is external Quality Assurance in place and the role documented		
4	Is there "one" Project Manager with overall responsibility for the Project or are there multiple Project Managers?		
5	Are there separate Team Managers in use where appropriate		

	Focus on Products		
1	Does the Project have a Project Product Description		
2	Are Product Descriptions being used effectively and include - Measurable quality criteria - Prioritised Quality Criteria - Quality tolerances - Quality responsibilities		
3	Is Product Based Planning being used to plan the Project, Stage and Work Package		
	Learn from Experience		
1	Are lessons being - Sought - Documented - Reported upon		
2	Are lessons logs being maintained and Lessons Reports being produced		
3	Are lessons from previous projects being captured and used within the planning process		
	Tailor to the Project		
1	Is the methodology being tailored to the organisation and project needs		
2	It terminology being adapted or adjusted		
3	Is the methodology adapted for simple\small\less complex projects		

Project Timeline – Example Project

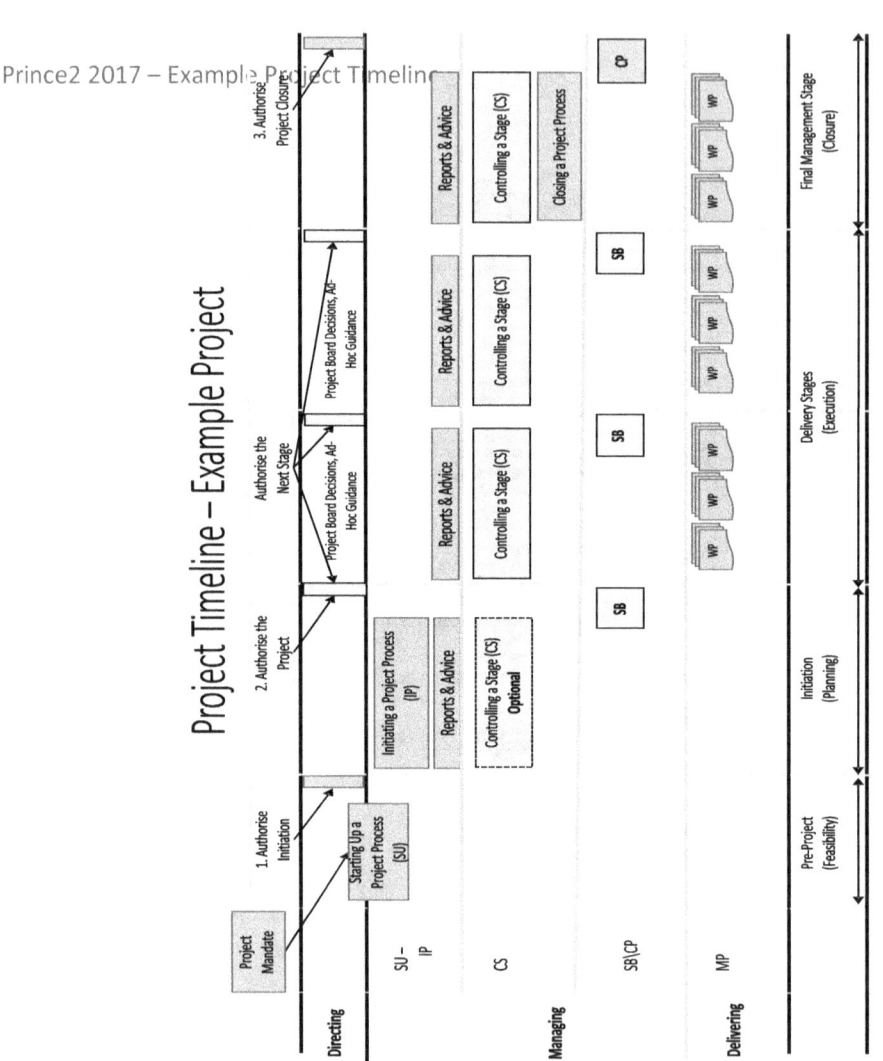

Prince2 2017 – Manual Tabs

Crucial

Principles	Theme Business Case	Theme Quality	Theme Quality	Theme Plans	Theme Risk	Theme Change	Theme Progress
P19	P44	P57	P77	P93	P119	P137	P147

Process Model	SU	DP	IP	CS	MP	SB	CP
P158	P165	P179	P195	P215	P235	P245	P259

Project Board	Executive	Senior User	Senior Supplier	Project Manager	Team Manager	Project Assurance	Change Authority	Project Support
P338	P340	P341	P341	P342	P344	P345	P347	P347

Optional

Benefits Management Approach	Business Case	Change Control Approach	Checkpoint Report	Communication Management Approach	Configuration Item record	Daily Log	End Project Report	End Stage Report	Exception Report
P292	P294	P296	P298	P299	P301	P301	P301	P303	P305

Highlight Report	Issue Register	Issue Report	Lessons Log	Lessons Report	Plan	Product Description	Product Status Account	Project Brief	PID	Project Product Description
P306	P308	P309	P311	P312	P313	P315	P317	P317	P319	P322

Quality Management Approach	Quality Register	Risk Management Approach	Risk Register	Work Package
P324	P325	P327	P329	P330

Directing a Project Process (DP)

Prince2 2017

No Management Products created or updated – Only Approvals\Authorizations or Ad-Hoc advice\Guidance

Starting Up A Project Process (SU)	Initiating a Project Process (IP)	Controlling a Stage Process (CS)	Managing Product Delivery (MP)	Managing a Stage Boundary Process (SB)	Closing a Project Process (CP)
Create - Daily Log Lessons Log Project Brief – 1. Project Definition 2. Project Approach 3. Project Management Role Descriptions 4. Project Management Team Structure 5. Outline Business Case 6. (Draft) Project Product Description Initiation Stage Plan	**Create -** Project Initiation Documentation (PID) 1. (Detailed) Business Case 2. Project Controls 3. Tailoring 4. Risk Management Approach 5. Change Control Approach 6. Quality Management Approach 7. Communication Management Approach Role Descriptions Risk register Issue Register Quality Register Configuration Item Records Benefits Management Approach	**Create –** Highlight Report Authorised Work Package Issue Report (as needed) Exception Report (as needed) **Review\Update -** Stage Plan Configuration Item Records Quality Register Risk Register Issue Register Work Package Lessons Log	**Create –** Team Plan Specialist Products Checkpoint Reports Approval Records **Review\Update -** Team Plan Stage Plan Configuration Item Records Quality Register Risk Register Issue Register Work Package Lessons Log	**Create -** (Next) Stage Plan New Product Descriptions End Stage Report (current Stage) Lessons Report (Optional) Follow-on Action Recommendations Exception Plan (as needed) **Review\Update -** PID (Contents of) Benefits Management Approach Project Plan Stage Plan Product Descriptions Configuration Item Records Quality Register Risk Register Issue Register Work Package Lessons Log	**Planned Closure** **Create –** Follow-on Action Recommendations End Project Report Lessons Report Draft Closure Notification **Premature Closure** **Create –** All above Additional Work Estimates **Review\Update -** Project Plan Configuration Item Records Benefits Management Approach **Close** Quality Register Risk Register Issue Register Daily Log Lessons Log